FOREWORD

This book is a revised and updated version of IN TUNE WITH INFINITE POWERS which I wrote in 2006. Since then my researches have continued and I realised that while my first book introduced many weird and wonderful concepts, there was no mention of how we might put these concepts to work to improve our daily lives. So now I have attempted to link the theory with the practical – like using dowsing for instance to give us information not available to our five senses. We live in a wonderful world, full of mysteries, and I hope this book will spur you to think in a different way which will make you part of this wonderful world and make this wonderful world part of you.

CONTENTS

Foreword

Preface

1   Strange powers   1

2   All the universe is energy   6

3   Under attack from the mind vampires   34

4   The Energy at work   65

5   Plugging into the Power   111

6   Using the power   139

7   Out of this world   164

8   The Ultimate Sceptic   179

9   A quick summary to take away   187

    Appendix   190

    About the author   201

    Bibliography   203

Paranormal | - Denoting events or phenomena such as telekinesis or clairvoyance that are beyond the scope of normal scientific understanding: a mystic who can prove he has paranormal powers

Psychic | 'sy kik| - Relating to or denoting faculties or phenomena that are apparently inexplicable by natural laws, esp. involving telepathy or clairvoyance : psychic powers (of a person) appearing or considered to have powers beyond the normal five senses: I could sense it - I must be psychic.

DEDICATION

I would like to thank all those kind readers who took the trouble to write a review on Amazon UK (every one rated as 5 star – thank you), of my second non-fiction book *Dowse Your Way To Psychic Power*. Here's what some of them said: 'Simply and intelligently written with great explanations and no jargon'...'I couldn't put it down until I came to the end...then I was sad I'd finished it!'...'The most interesting book on dowsing I have found so far'...'an absolute must for anyone interested in rebalancing their lives'...'Thank you, Anthony. Would love to read more in depth books by you in the future...' I hope *In Tune With The Infinite Mind* will live up to their, and your, expectations.

PREFACE

'There's a Divinity that shapes our ends, rough-hew them how we will' – Shakespeare's Hamlet

Do you believe in synchronicity? That is, co-incidences that are timely and meaningful. Could it be that this book has found you just when you need it? If you feel your life is heading in the wrong direction, suspend your disbelief, reach for a higher awareness and read on to the end and then decide what is right for you. Just knowing the information that this book contains will change the forces in your life.

Every day the world is sliding further into chaos. Dark Forces are gathering strength. You can see this but why can't everyone else? But there is something you can do. These same powers that are being drawn upon to propagate terrorism, hatred and fear are not partisan. They are equally capable of being used to enhance our lives. Electricity can light a bulb or kill.

What are these powers? Where do they come from? The purpose of this book is to explore these questions. One thing to bear in mind, though, is that when we come to dealing with matters outside the normal realms of perception we are up against the barrier of language. Sometimes words are inadequate to explain the inexplicable.

1 STRANGE POWERS

INTERCONNECTIONS, CONSCIOUSNESS EXPLOSION, COSMIC SYMPHONY, RESONANCES, ANOMALOUS PHENOMENA, THEORY OF FORMATIVE CAUSATION, COSMOGENIC ENERGY, MY EUREKA! MOMENT

How do you describe colours to a person blind from birth? Or a Beethoven symphony to someone who has never been able to hear? All you can do is use metaphors that will have some relevance in their world. But even then the picture will at times be shrouded in fog.

How much more difficult then to discuss occurrences, entities, phenomena, realms, dimensions, anomalous behaviours and so on beyond the normal limits of our understanding? All we can do is select metaphoric approximations and leave it to our minds to make some sense of it.

All things past, present and future are everywhere. In us,

through us and around us existing in different dimensions. We are inter-connected with everything - to the end of eternity. Our every thought reverberates around the cosmos, affecting it for ever. The human consciousness has a power beyond our understanding. Everything from the most distant star to our own bodies and minds are made of discrete packets of energy with their own, unique frequencies, harmonising in one, eternal celestial symphony. Every molecule of our beings is playing notes heard across the heavens.

We influence 'out there' and 'out there' influences us, which is where inspiration, music, art, inventions, new ideas come from.

We are on the verge of a consciousness explosion that will propel humankind onto the next level of evolution and each life has a unique part to play in this cosmic plan.

The wonder of all this is obscured by our mechanistic view of life in which what we can see, hear, touch, smell and taste dominates. It is the world of the so-called paranormal that reminds us that we are surrounded by powers that exist beyond our five senses but which can and do have a profound effect on our daily lives. In fact, without our realising it, these powers are manipulating us in a never-ending battle of psychic wills.

When I first began writing these words I found myself having to argue the logic of my theories with a 'voice' in my head pooh-poohing many things I was writing. I was tempted to try to shut the voice out and grimly plough on. Then I thought, 'Wait a minute, maybe something 'out there' is deliberately acting the role of Devil's Advocate to test the strength of my case'.

So, I decided to include the voice's viewpoint in a series of Questions & Answers at the end of each section. I hope they serve to answer some of your questions, too.

Just as radio and TV signals are invisible but you know they are there, there are resonances all around us. These resonances convey mysterious forces that some scientists reluctantly agree are there but have yet to be proved under laboratory conditions.

However, clues can be found in psychic and anomalous phenomena, the effects of which are there for all eyes to see and wonder at. Take poltergeists, for instance. For centuries, thousands of rational, sane people around the world have witnessed apparently miraculous happenings associated with these 'noisy ghosts,' which have defied explanation. Somehow, energy is being manipulated by unseen forces in a way that cannot be reproduced, despite the best efforts of 21st Century science.

Similar Strange Powers are associated with anomalous happenings like faith healing, dowsing, curses, telepathy, precognition, clairvoyance, levitation, plant 'awareness', mathematical prodigies, possession, Multiple Personality Disorder (now re-named Dissociative Identity Disorder) and time shifts.

A lifetime of studying these phenomena, allied to Dr Rupert Sheldrake's Theory of Formative Causation and some aspects of Quantum Physics, has convinced me that we are being influenced by forces all around us which either have an intelligence of their own or are being manipulated by some kind of intelligence.

We humans arrogantly believe that we are in control of our own destinies, while in fact we are being buffeted daily by influences we are not even aware of. In many ways we are like pieces on a chessboard being moved about by some kind of cosmic Grand Master. But, it is possible to regain control and harness these forces, which collectively I call Cosmogenic Energy.

While the 'Grand Master' knows the future, reality is unfolding like some celestial drama with each of us conjuring each scene with our free will. But the choices we make are already known. If you find it difficult to get your head round all this just go with the flow for a bit as explanations will unfold as you read on.

My journey into the world of the Unexplained began with a casual interest in psychic happenings. The more I read, the more intrigued I became. An amazing variety of strange goings-on occur every day in some part of the world. But, apart from causing a mild interest, it does not change our lives. Tabloid newspapers print sensational stories, which are quickly overshadowed by the latest celebrity sex scandal or some other lurid story.

But, to me, those accounts of UFOs, Out Of Body Experiences, angels and demons, precognition, elementals, other dimensions, reincarnation and so on provided intriguing glimpses of other worlds where our laws of physics seem not to apply.

Respected researchers have authenticated many of the manifestations but no-one has been able to explain the Hows? And the Whys? How do solid objects like stones or gold rings materialise and de-materialise in poltergeist activity or at séances? How can a body defy gravity and levitate? How can a child of six beat a computer in complex mathematical calculations?

So started 40 years of research that took me on a labyrinthine trek down the highways and byways of the weird and wonderful. Gradually, I refined my analyses and was intrigued to note that there were some common threads linking disparate phenomena. I found important clues in the work of some of humankind's greatest minds, ranging from Albert Einstein to biologist Dr Rupert Sheldrake.

Then a Eureka! Moment occurred and I was sure I had discovered the psi equivalent of Einstein's Theory of Relativity. There followed a journey through space, time and other dimensions. My mind whirled with arcane theories like Heisenberg's Uncertainty Principle, the Einstein – Podolski – Rosen Paradox and the Interference Pattern.

What I hope this book will prove to you is that the Universe is energy and thought is energy and that our minds are engaged in an eternal struggle with negative forces and this is a major contributory factor to the increasing world chaos of the 21st century. But we – you - can fight back.

If what follows prompts you to take up the challenge of harnessing these energies, you could precipitate a consciousness explosion and nudge the world towards its next evolutionary step and a better place.

Thought worth pondering: Stop the mind and learn the truth

'After years of thought, study and contemplation I have come to the conclusion that there is only one thing in the universe and that is energy – beyond that there is a supreme intelligence' – Albert Einstein

2 ALL THE UNIVERSE IS ENERGY

COSMIC CONSCIOUSNESS, ZPF, DARK MATTER, QUANTUM UNIVERSE, THOUGHT POWER, HEISENBERG'S UNCERTAINTY PRINCIPLE, DOUBLE-SLIT EXPERIMENT.

Although he had come to realize that there were holes in his Theory of Relativity, at the end of his life Einstein was convinced of one thing: the universe is composed of energy and that there seemed to be an intelligence at work orchestrating this energy into one, continuous cosmic symphony.

Controlling our universal orchestra is a mystical conductor. Nothing, nothing happens by accident. Every one of us is born to a purpose and every moment we live contributes to that cosmic masterwork. The future is known;

humanity is shaping it to be what has already been decreed. As Shakespeare said in As You Like It, 'All the world's a stage and all the men and women merely players.'

Thought is energy and energy follows thought. The universe is thought and thoughts are subtle vibrations permeating everything. These energies exist across many parallel dimensions and planes of being which have their own laws, but which sometimes overlap with ours; in fact we are all living in an invisible, resonating 'soup' of vibrations that shade into one another like the electromagnetic spectrum.

Our daily lives tend to be limited to a narrow part of that bandwidth - tunnel vision in a landscape of unbelievable colour and excitement.

Our ability to 'tune in' to these frequencies is limited only by our scepticism and our mental bunkers which, while keeping us locked safely away from unwanted intrusion, stops us from fulfilling our true destiny.

The key to tapping into these energies lies in our mind, which is a powerful transmitting and receiving system reaching out into the Infinite. This is an analogy that we need to accept for the time being in order to better understand the theories that will unfold as we journey together through these writings. However, later we shall see that 'transmitting' and 'receiving' is not what is actually happening.

But to get back to setting the scene. What we create in our minds becomes an energy reality from that moment on and has the ability to take on a life of its own, affecting the world around it for good or evil. Whatever your mind gives out will join similar energies gathering like clouds jostling for ascendancy.

We live in exciting times. Never before has there been an era when baffling anomalous happenings and the disciplined world of science have so come close to merging.

By their very nature, scientists need to have proof. Unless something can be captured, measured, manipulated and controlled in laboratory conditions, the scientific community will not admit that it exists. The universe is full of forces that are invisible but some are measurable. These forces have a discernible effect on the world around us and scientists are content to admit as much, so long as they have proof.

In the electromagnetic spectrum, for instance, there are frequencies that carry radio and television transmissions, there are microwaves, far infrared, infrared, visible light, ultraviolet light, x-rays and, from thousands of light years away, gamma rays.

Then there are the elusive neutrinos. These are the tiny, energetic particles with neither mass nor electric charge which originate from the far reaches of the Cosmos. Apparently, a hundred trillion neutrinos pass through our bodies every second. Some even penetrate giant clouds of interstellar gas and dust and travel on through the Earth, without leaving a trace. Some scientists believe that the lower-energy neutrinos may comprise a large proportion of the mass in the universe.

And we must not forget Dark Matter - that invisible, mysterious collection of something that holds the universe together. It's another of those insoluble aspects of astrophysics that cosmologists have confined to the 'too difficult' tray in their labs. They know it exists because its gravity bends the light of stars and galaxies as they hurtle on their way. Dark Matter makes up about 90 per cent of the universe and seems to have a force that holds everything in place, rather like a fly is held in amber.

But pushing everything apart is its opposite number - Dark Energy, a mysterious force that, again, no one understands. In his so-called 'cosmological constant' Einstein included such an 'anti-gravity' effect in his Theory of General Relativity. But while everyone went along with the theory no-one, including Einstein himself, took it very seriously. Now, it's popped up thumbing its nose and saying it's here to stay whether we like it or not, causing quite an upset for astronomers who have to adjust to an unexpected and outlandish new view of the universe.

'I'm as big a fan of dark matter and dark energy as anybody else,' says astronomer Richard Ellis of Caltech. 'But', he adds, 'I find it very worrying that you have a universe where there are three constituents, of which only one, ordinary matter, is really physically understood.'

And co-existing with both Dark Matter and Dark Energy is the Zero Point Field - the source of limitless and inconceivable amounts of energy. One cupful, say the scientists, would contain enough energy to boil away every ocean of the world.

Exactly what is ZPF?

It is standard in quantum theory to apply something called the Heisenberg Uncertainty Principle (more on this later – don't groan! Stick with it, it will be worth it I promise) which, basically, says that while you can measure the position at any one time of a sub-atomic particle like an electron, you cannot at the same time measure its speed. This is because it jiggles about all the time. The same applies to electric and magnetic fields which oscillate as they flow through space.

At every possible frequency there will always be some electromagnetic jiggling going on. And if you add up all these ceaseless fluctuations, what you get is a background sea of light whose total energy is enormous: the zero-point field.

The 'zero-point' refers to the fact that even though this energy is huge, it is the lowest possible energy state. All other energy is over and above the zero-point state. Take any volume of space and take away everything else - in other words, create a vacuum - and what you are left with is the zero-point field.

We can imagine a true vacuum, devoid of everything, but the real-world quantum vacuum is permeated by the zero-point field with its ceaseless electromagnetic jumpings and jerkings.

At this point you are beginning to get the message that, whatever you might like to call it, there is a ceaseless activity of invisible energies churning on around us wherever we are. And this ceaseless churning is also happening on the other side of the universe billions of light years away.

And this concoction of frequencies is what makes up our Cosmogenic Energy. No measuring instrument has yet been invented that can define its properties but, nevertheless, the evidence is there even though it cannot, yet, be confirmed in the laboratory. But, our minds know it is there and both consciously and unconsciously we utilise its forces. In fact, systems theorist Ervin Lazlo says the ZPF is actually the storage facility for all our memories and that the mind is merely a retrieval and read-out mechanism linked to it. This is a scientist's version of the Buddhist belief that everything that has happened and will happen is recorded in an invisible Cosmic library. This was later adopted by the founder of the Theosophy movement, Rudolph Steiner.

The evidence for a force (or forces) 'out there' is all around us and has been since the beginning of time. Now at last, with the advent of the Quantum Universe, scientists are reluctantly having to accept phenomena that up to the 20th Century would have been ridiculed and relegated to the world of magicians and alchemists.

The manifestations of the quantum world are out of this world. Those of us for whom the quantum realm is the stuff of frizzy-haired geniuses can take heart. Frizzy-haired geniuses don't know what's going on either. But something remarkable is happening, the greater understanding of which could change human destiny. And you are part of it.

Incidentally, the word quanta in connection with physics was first coined by German physicist Max Planck who proposed that energy might come in discrete bites or quanta. For example atoms of light, or photons, are quanta.

Quantum physics has turned conventional thinking on its head, has baffled Einstein and has created the possibility of a linkage between quantum events and the human mind. Yes, the microscopic worlds of sub-atomic particles and psychic phenomena are converging.

Physics began as a science when Isaac Newton and others

discovered that mathematics could accurately describe the observed world. Today the Newtonian view of physics is referred to as classical physics; in essence, classical physics is a mathematical confirmation of common sense. It makes four basic assumptions about the fabric of reality that correspond more or less to how the world appears to our senses. These assumptions are reality, locality, causality, and continuity.

Reality means that irrespective of whether we can see and feel it the physical world is objectively real and there anyway. Locality refers to the idea that objects need a physical influence to make them move.

Causality follows on from this and states that a cause will be followed by an effect (you fire a gun and the bullet will leave the muzzle). Continuity assumes that time moves forward smoothly and in one direction.

Classical physics is common sense physics; a clockwork, billiard ball universe that we can readily understand. Quantum physics is Alice Through The Looking Glass physics. In this world reality can be in two places at once, locality can be pushed by an invisible hand, causality arranges for the bullet to arrive before the gun is fired and continuity jumps dizzyingly back and forth in time and space.

Back to Heisenberg and his Uncertainty Principle for a moment. Way back in 1927 he said of sub atomic particles like the electron: 'The more precisely the position is determined, the less precisely the momentum is known in this instant, and vice versa.'

This became known as his Uncertainty Principle and its acceptance by the scientific community meant the acceptance of the seemingly magical world of quantum mechanics.

As, in a Quantum Mechanical world, you cannot predict where a particle will be with 100 per cent certainty physicists speak in terms of probabilities. For example, you can calculate that an atom will be at some location with a 99 per cent probability, but there will be a 1 per cent possibility it will be somewhere else - even across the other side of the Universe. These particles can appear in places where they have no right to be as far as classical physics is concerned.

And this weird behaviour of the sub-atomic realm deeply offended Albert Einstein. While Einstein had proved that, at 186,000 miles per second, light is the fastest thing in the universe, he became distinctly uneasy at the 'action-at-a-distance' evidenced in so-called 'quantum entanglement' where, unbelievably, two particles separated by vast distances could affect one another in an instant with no time lag for travel.

For example, 'orders' changing the polarity of one entangled particle would somehow be communicated to the other at a speed apparently faster than light. Einstein couldn't accept this, or the other uncertainties introduced by quantum theory. 'God does not play dice with the universe,' he famously wrote to his friend and physicist Max Born. 'Oh yes he does,' theoretical cosmologist, Dr Stephen Hawking, said long after Einstein's death. And added, 'On the contrary, it appears that not only does God play dice, but also that He sometimes throws the dice where they can't be seen.'

In Einstein's well-ordered domain (which we ordinary human beings find comforting) things travel from A to B, cause precedes effect and energies transform from one state to another via a logical sequence. Einstein's orthodox view was that sub-nuclear particles behaved like bullets fired from a gun. However, according to quantum physics pioneer Neils Bohr electrons from an electron gun 'simply turn up at the target.' It was this Alice-Through-The-Looking-Glass stuff that drove Einstein to distraction (and this is where we might later argue that thoughts etc are not transmitted and received but just 'turn up').

In particular, Einstein did not like the connectedness proposition. He just could not conceive of 'action at a distance.' It violated his principle of 'local realism' which states that changes performed on one physical system should have no immediate effect on another, spatially-separated system. He told his colleagues that the 'spooky' connectedness of particles was a reason why quantum theory had to be wrong.

With two younger colleagues, Boris Podolski and Nathan Rosen, he attempted experiments, which ultimately failed, to disprove what apparently was going on. Their efforts became known as the Einstein-Podolski-Rosen, or EPR, paradox.

However, a detailed analysis of the EPR experiment shows that while quantum mechanics does violate locality, it does not infringe the principle of causality, because no information is actually *transmitted* in the phenomena of quantum entanglement.

The core mystery of the whole thing is that, somehow, one particle twin 'knows' what affects the other and instantly changes itself accordingly. How? No-one has a clue. It's magic. But it's an important clue to support the theory that everything in the universe is interconnected. To make it easier for my own brain I think of it as two ends of an infinitely long iron rod. If you twist one end, the other end turns with no gap of time in between because the two ends are both part of one thing – the rod.

After Einstein's death John Bell at CERN, the European laboratory for particle physics near Geneva, Switzerland, proved that two particles did remain linked in a ghostly and inexplicable way. In his experiments, twin particles seemed joined as if at the ends of my invisible rod, even one a million miles long. The two particles formed an inseparable ensemble, even though they might be infinitely distant.

This fact opens up sweeping implications. Is the universe a vast collection of linked and interacting particles? And are we all part of one quantum system?

Our frizzy-haired scientists are being driven mad trying to make sense of it all. Their wilder hypotheses include: Does the first particle measured go back in time to warn its twin of the state that it must adopt? Does there exist a sort of instantaneous telepathy between particles? Is there an 'indivisible totality' of the Universe?

One of the most fundamental pieces of research that has thrown die-hard classical scientists into disarray is the celebrated Double Slit Experiment. Hold onto your hats because the implications of this experiment led to my Eureka! Moment. The Double Slit Experiment is where light is shone at a screen with two parallel slits cut in it. This causes an outline of light and dark strips to be formed on another screen behind. These strips of light and dark are called an interference pattern, caused by light spreading out from the two slits in a series of overlapping waves.

However, when photons - single particles of light (think

of little marbles) are fired at the slits there should be no pattern as there are no waves to 'interfere' with each other. But, inexplicably, there is still an interference pattern reflected on the wall. How can this be when there are no waves to overlap? Experimenters concluded that single photons seemed to be able to go through two slits at the same time. This meant that each particle has a ghostly twin in another universe mimicking its every move.

Even more incredibly, it also seems as if the photons can read the experimenters' minds because, as each single photon is fired, the interference effect builds up on the screen according to a pattern anticipated by the human watchers! Also, scientists found that the particles seemed to know that they were being watched and adjusted their behaviour accordingly. When physicists tested for the presence of particles they got particles; when they tested for light waves, they got waves. It seems that the test itself tried to oblige the humans involved by determining a result they desired, which is utterly alien to classical physics.

I know this seems crazy, but stay with it because things get even weirder.

Confirming that there seems to be an apparent intelligence at work, the particles become overtly coy when the experiment is taken on a stage. When the experimenters set up a detector to measure which slit each particle goes through, the photons refused to behave like waves and remained as particles creating one spot on the screen as one might expect. As soon as the detector is switched off, the particles resume behaving like waves, creating an interference pattern!

One conclusion that could be drawn is that the mind of

man creates reality. But there is another deduction even more fundamental.

According to American physicist Richard Feynman, the unexplained behaviour of photons and electrons applies to all sub-atomic particles and the Double Slit Experiment goes to the core of the quantum mystery (there is an excellent visual explanation of the Double Slit Experiment on YouTube. Just follow this link: http://bit.ly/1NILGUI

A further refinement of the experiment takes us into the realms of the profound and provides the basis for answers to metaphysical questions like What is life for? Why are we here? If there is a God why does he allow suffering? This refinement of the experiment is known as Delayed Choice. Here, a detector is set up between the two screens to monitor the particular route a particle is taking AFTER it has passed through the slits but BEFORE it hits the screen. Remember, if the particle 'thinks' it is being monitored it remains a photon resulting in a blob of light on the screen. However, if it is not being monitored it is quite happy to behave like a wave and go through two slits at the same time.

By setting up the monitor between the screens, theoretically it will be too late for the particle to decide whether to be a photon or a wave, as it will already have made the choice and gone through the slit. Amazingly though, when the monitor is switched on the particle remains a particle and when switched off the particle behaves like a wave and creates a typical interference pattern. This means that the photon already knows what mode the monitor will be in BEFORE it passes through the slit. How? Does it read the experimenters' minds? Can it tell the future?

These experiments were conducted independently of each other by the University of Maryland in the US and the University of Munich in Germany.

If you extrapolate these results to a cosmic scale, and use two beams of diffracted light from a star millions of light years away, the particles and waves would behave in the same way by appearing on your screen as blobs of light or an interference pattern, depending on whether your monitor was switched on or off. Which means that, as the light from the star has taken millions of years to arrive on earth, it must have 'known' when it first began its journey that it was going to be monitored. Before the human species had even begun to evolve. How? Does this support the argument of Predestination? That everything is pre-ordained by a Creator for whom we are just playthings?

So the quantum universe has thrown up paradoxes and weirdnesses that rival anything the world of the paranormal can manage. Some scientists try to explain it by suggesting that there could be an infinite number of realities which exist alongside our own. Every choice of life is made within these other realities and our lives progress according to our choices, which creates our reality. So, you might marry, have children and divorce in this life whereas in the universe next door you might remain single and in the parallel world next to that you might die as a child. The Universe is a seething mass of probabilities and only human consciousness can 'conjure' any of those probabilities into reality.

And, part of our consciousness that exists outside ourselves (the mind?) pursues at a quantum level the choices we did not make, giving part of us an existence in all the other parallel worlds in which the infinite number of options are being played out. Whether you go along with this theory or not, it is another pointer to our minds and thoughts having powerful effects on the world (and worlds) about us. Or do they?

Some philosophers believe that our human consciousness actually influences quantum events, which could be argued is a logical extension of the Delayed Choice result. This mind over matter idea is the basis of Danish physicist Neils Bohr's Copenhagen Interpretation: that there is no meaning to the objective existence of a quantum particle unless it is observed. Until you see it, it isn't there. He used to say that if people did not find what he was telling them absolutely amazing, they were not taking it in.

The 'nothing exists until it's observed' theory is illustrated by the famous - or infamous - so-called Schrodinger's cat experiment, proposed by Erwin Schrodinger in 1935 to demonstrate something called the quantum theory of superposition.

Schrodinger's cat demonstrates the apparent conflict between what quantum theory tells us is true about the nature and behaviour of matter on the microscopic level and what we can see to be be true about the nature and behaviour of matter on the macroscopic level.

Schrodinger, who later in life confessed he wished he'd never met the damned cat, said that if you place a theoretical cat in a thick lead box subsequent events would clearly show what he meant by superposition of states.

When the cat goes into the box it is perfectly healthy.

However, in with it you place a cyanide capsule which will break at the slightest touch. From then on we don't know if the cat is alive or if it has broken the vial and died. Since we don't know, the cat is in the 'superposition' of being both dead and alive at the same time. It is only when we break open the box and learn the condition of the cat that the superposition is lost, and the cat becomes either dead or alive.

With our Double Slit Experiment we know that superposition actually occurs at the subatomic level, because there are observable effects of interference, in which a single particle is demonstrated to be in multiple locations simultaneously. But, in the reality we see around us can the cat be both dead and alive? When and how does the model of many microscopic possibilities resolve itself into a particular macroscopic state? That is the measurement problem and Schrodinger's cat is a simple and elegant explanations of that problem. Our frizzie-haired scientists admit this is still one of the stickiest areas of quantum physics.

The American philosopher Danah Zohar, wife of British psychiatrist Ian Marshall, believes that consciousness is the bridge between classical physics and the quantum world. She believes our consciousness makes us co-creators of the universe we're part of. This is also the belief of John Wheeler, a towering figure in the world of theoretical physics (see Appendix 1). This concept is used by doctors in a Beijing medicineless hospital. Western medics witnessed a cancerous growth just dissolve before their eyes. Doctors working in the hospital explained they didn't judge the cancer good or bad – it was just a 'quantum possibility' of which there were many and this was just one of them.

They explained that having acknowledged this fact they would decide to 'choose another one.' Unlike their conventional colleagues who were trained to manipulate the cancer, these quantum doctors used their minds to change the quantum blueprint of the patient, allowing their feelings to assume another possibility had occurred which replaced the cancer. In this procedure they had accessed the realm in which all possibilities exist simultaneously and had made a different choice. Ancient cultures, which knew nothing about the quantum world, would do exactly the same thing by reaching into these possibilities with their minds and choosing one.

One of quantum mechanics' shortcomings is that it doesn't truly explain how reality emerges from the quantum world of elementary particles and probability waves. Zohar believes that the answer has always been in the theory, and that we should simply take it at face value.

She subscribes to the thesis of Bose-Einstein condensation advocated by Ian Marshall which, basically, equates mind/body duality to wave/particle duality. She believes that the self does change all the time, quantum interference making each new self sprout from the old selves.

In her ground-breaking book *The Quantum Self* she substitutes the saga of Schrodinger's Cat for the fortunes of a 'Cosmic Hussy' who experiences all the possible paths that a young girl might take from virginity to wedded bliss. Her heroine selects, simultaneously, all of her possible suitors and lives out her life with each one, marrying, having children and grandchildren, before finally settling on one partner.

Thus, she demonstrates the parallel selves we all are, one of which happens to be the life we recognise as 'now.'

However, our other selves have significantly influenced 'out there.'

Zohar proposes that '. . . mind is relationship and matter is that to which it relates. Neither, on its own, could evolve or express anything; together they give us ourselves and the world.'

She said, 'I discovered quantum physics at 15, and it stood my whole world on its head. The ways things are based in Newtonian physics differ from those based in the quantum physics paradigm has been the whole substance of my work and runs through it completely.

'Newtonian physics conceives of the universe essentially as little billiard balls, atoms with hard boundaries. According to this principle, there's no way to change an atom - scientists in the early days didn't know about subatomic particles or any of the things that have so radically changed our way of understanding nature. In the Newtonian model, when two of these billiard balls meet, they bump into each other and knock each other off course, but neither changes the other.

'Quantum systems, on the other hand, are thought to be concretized balls of energy that take on different forms as they relate to each other through participating in the system together. When two quantum systems meet, they overlap and combine their total identity. All the patterns of dynamic energy within these systems change dramatically in relation to each other, leading to the emergence of a whole new thing that is greater than the sum of its parts.'

Scientists have attempted to rationalise all conflicting conundrums either in terms of classical or quantum physics.

They have been mentally wrestling with the paradoxes - effect before cause, entanglement phenomena happening faster than the speed of light, particles that 'anticipate' what is required of them. Theories to explain the anomalies range from particles that read minds, or go back in time or predict the future. Even though these ideas are the stuff of science fiction, at least they make a sort of sense.

But how about a different theory? Could it be that the Cosmic Consciousness, or the Universal Mind, or whatever you want to call some kind of over-arching intelligence, already 'knows' what human consciousness is to bring into being in the future. As it has already brought into being the past and the present. So, in a sense, the past, present and future already exists because the 'knowing' has created it.

This chimes in with the quantum universe's propensity to have an effect BEFORE the cause. The future is already there because it is known but it is yet to be 'conjured' up. And that is why particles 'know' when they are being watched. Whether they are to form a pattern on a screen, or not, is already 'known.' So they are not reading the scientists' minds. Rather they are behaving as they are obliged to behave to fulfil their part in the future. What all this boils down to is the question: Are we just puppets playing out our lives according to a 'script' already written? What about Free Will? I hear you cry.

The scientists' decisions whether or not to monitor the particles is still a matter of free choice but the outcome is already in place (in the Universal Mind's knowledge of the future) in anticipation of their decisions. Both the scientists and the particles are participating in a grand cosmic drama which is unfolding as directed by the Universal Consciousness.

That is why the light waves from a star can 'know' what would be in a scientist's mind millions of light years in the future. The result is already in place (effect) but the choice (cause) has yet to be made.

Mankind is living out its destiny complying with a meticulously created, ghostly, scenario known already to the Universal Mind, but yet to be brought to life. The birth and death of universes, stretching across millions of light years and encompassing billions of galaxies, is following the same principle. Energies, frequencies, resonances have 'created' events and now the human race is adding its contribution.

This concept is awesome. If the feeling of individual insignificance when looking up on a starry night is overwhelming, remember that even the most humble of human lives is making a significant contribution to an eternal celestial act of creation. Yes, you, sitting in your lonely bed-sit wondering whether anyone cares and you couldn't blame them if they don't because your worthless anyway. No, no, no...You are definitely not worthless. You are essential for completion of the Master Plan, of which we humble humans can only see a fraction. No, you don't need to go out and do good works. No you don't have to hold the fate of nations in your hands. You are important by just being you.

On his 1971 trip home from the moon, Apollo 14 astronaut Edgar Mitchell had a life-changing epiphany. As he watched planet Earth floating in the vastness of space he was engulfed by a profound sense of universal connectedness. In Mitchell's own words: 'The presence of divinity became almost palpable, and I knew that life in the universe was not just an accident based on random processes...The knowledge came to me directly.'

He later played a significant role in supporting the scientific investigation of consciousness. The view he had of the Earth from space gave him deep insights into the creative nature of consciousness in the universe:

'In one moment I realized that this universe is intelligent. It is proceeding in a direction and we have something to do with that direction. And that creative spirit, the creative intent that has been the history of this planet, comes from within us, and it is out there - it is all the same...Consciousness itself is what is fundamental and energy-matter is the product of consciousness...

'If we change our heads about who we are - and can see ourselves as creative, eternal beings creating physical experience, joined at that level of existence we call consciousness - then we start to see and create this world that we live in quite differently.'

Mitchell's mystical insights led him to believe that the creativity inherent in the universe is also within us. His vision suggests that we may play a vital role as participants in the creative process of the life of the whole Earth. These insights were later echoed by the research of consciousness theorists and physicists Peter Russell and Amit Goswami.

Mitchell, Russell and Goswami offer a view of how the whole universe at its most fundamental level is consciousness, and that the consciousness that permeates the universe dwells within each of us. We become aware of this through altered states like meditation.

Mitchell went on to found the Institute of Noetic Sciences, which explores the inner cosmos of the mind - consciousness, soul, spirit - and how it relates to the outer cosmos of the physical world. Here's a link to IONS: http://noetic.org/

This whole concept of a universal inter-connectedness is exciting and liberating. There is, after all, a meaning to everything. There is a destiny that is unfolding and we are part of it. Each individual is a fundamental component of a Grand Plan. While we retain our free will and must make our own choices, the future we are shaping is a future that is already 'there.'

Q: You won't be surprised to know that I've got a few questions. For a start, at least the boffins' madcap ideas have some logic. But you ask us to believe the past, present and future is already there, like some theatrical performance. But that this theatrical performance won't happen until thoughts, human or otherwise, create it. If this is the case, doesn't it mean that people are just robots, carrying out a function, with no real free will?

A: Not really. Although everything is pre-known, and therefore a reality already in the mind of the Supreme Consciousness, we as human beings can't know what that reality is, so we are free to make individual choices.

Q: But how can we be free to make individual choices, say between good and evil, positive or negative, if the outcome's already been decided? Like those experimenters' decisions whether to monitor or not to monitor. According to you, their thoughts are their own but the particles already know what those thoughts are going to be and react in advance.

A: The outcome hasn't been decided in the sense that a scriptwriter is setting it all out in advance. But because the outcome is known it is a thought reality. So, while the particles are destined to create an interference pattern, or not, in accordance with the scientists' thoughts, the experimenters don't know what result they are going to achieve, so to all intents and purposes they are making a free choice, even though the outcome might be a pre-known one. Your choices are not pre-programmed but they bring into being the outcome, which is already there in the mind of the Supreme Being.

Q: Taking a step back for a second. If human beings conjure up their own futures by selecting from thoughts in their heads, where do these thoughts come from?

A: A good question. In fact a fundamental question. Where do thoughts come from? All thoughts, which range from how to split the atom to what vegetables to buy for supper, are 'out there' floating among the resonances responding to each person's unique frequency. They drop into your head and your brain makes a choice - good or bad, positive or negative, angelic or satanic. The 'you' is what you have become after you have made your choice.

Q: Are you saying that, however mundane the thought, it's put into my head by some cosmic puppeteer who then leaves it to me? Like, if I decide to go to the supermarket this is already ordained, as is what I buy, but that my choice is somehow free, even though the outcome is certain?

A: Yes. All thoughts are floating about in the Cosmogenic Field and arrive in your head offering you a choice of how you live your life. The thoughts you select are completely up to you and they are the ones that decide your future - from going to the theatre to moving house to getting a divorce. The outcome is the reality you create by having selected those thoughts.

Q: If you say the reality that actually happens is already 'written in the stars' as it were how can it be the reality I create?

A: Your choice of thought and action is free but, to the Universal Life Force, your choices are already known and the outcome is already there in the Matrix that makes up space and time. In other words, we are free to think our thoughts but their effect is already in place ready to happen. The freedom to choose is the difference between each one of us being a machine or a human being with self-determination.

Q: How can we have self-determination and be in charge of our own destinies, if the outcome's a one-way bet?

A: As I said, we can't see into the future so our thoughts and actions are not determined by what will happen but what might happen. On a less mundane level than the weekly shopping, that same puppeteer (although I like to think of it as a Universal Consciousness) already knows the fate of nations, civilisations and even stars and all our thoughts, inventions, scientific breakthroughs, artistic creations and every aspect of our lives are working towards fulfilling that Eternal Plan. That puppet-master outside of ourselves is who/what we interact with, and who knows the outcome based on that interaction.

Q: When you say all our thoughts, inventions etc are working towards a pre-known destiny isn't this the same as admitting we humans are just playthings of the gods and have no say, or control, over our futures. Voltaire said that we are all toys in the hands of Destiny.

A: Let me say again, we may all be participating in a cosmic drama but how each scene unfolds is known only to the playwright. Therefore, as we are confronted with the need to make decisions, we are free to make those decisions in line with our morality, motivations, needs or whatever conditions face us at the time. The fact that every decision we make, every action we take, is already known, does not invalidate the choices we make.

Q: OK. Let me take another example. I'm a mugger high on drugs and desperate for money. There's an old lady alone in the street ahead of me so I knock her down and grab her handbag. This is all part of the drama. It's bound to happen so I don't bother with my conscience because it was going to happen anyway?

A: Yes and No.

Q: Could you flesh that out a bit please?

A: Yes, the outcome of your encounter would have been known but No, you don't ignore your conscience. You could have made the decision not to mug the old lady.

Q: Sorry, but if it was already decreed that the old lady was going to be mugged by me what difference would it have made if I had listened to my conscience because she still would have been mugged.

A: Not necessarily. The cosmic script could have had the old lady being helped safely across a busy road by you and not mugged at all. The whole point is - and this is central to the predestination theory - you don't know what is in the future. The old lady might be destined to be mugged or helped across the road. The important thing is you had a choice BEFORE the future unfolded. And it's these choices we all make that mould us as individuals and create the history of nations.

Q: Are you saying that the only thing that matters as far as the human species on this earth is concerned is what we become as a result of our thoughts, words and deeds along the way?

A: I believe that we are all individual forms of energy and as such are indestructible. Our bodies may die but that eternal part of ourselves, our spirits if you like, has a role to play in whatever dimensions there are that exist outside of this one. Our time on this plane gives us each an opportunity to experience good and bad, positive and negative and think thoughts, make decisions and take actions according to our circumstances. Every moment that passes has an effect on that eternal part of ourselves, which will have a bearing on what part we play in the future in this cosmic drama.

Q: So according to you wars, terrorism, starvation, aids, natural disasters, man's inhumanity to man, is already in a celestial script and there's nothing we can do about it?

A: No, no, no. There is something we can do. We can make choices that avoid wars and terrorism. The celestial script, as you put it, is not being written by one all-powerful Being. Both good and bad forces are writing the lines and then trying to get us to play the appropriate parts. While over and above all that the Universal Mind does know the outcome, it is us who are bringing reality into being.

Q: You mean, stopping a war could be pre-destined too?

A: Yes, as could ending disease, poverty, hatred, envy and all the other ills of mankind. The Universal Mind knows what your thoughts are going to be (although you don't) and has already created the outcome.

Q: Sorry to labour the point but if everything's been conceived by some divine, or satanic, intelligence what on earth's the point of it all?

A: It seems to me that, in this life, the point is to give humanity the chance to develop and grow. If there are existences outside and beyond this plane what we have learned, and become, continue to make a contribution to the Eternal Plan.

Q: If this intelligence has got the vastness of the universe to play with, why is it bothering with something as insignificant as us?

A: Well, it's clear that it does and that human beings have been cast as central characters in the cosmic drama. In fact some scientists say that the precise balance of life-creating conditions in our solar system is proof that the Creator of all things wanted (and now needs) humans to exist.

Q: Some of what you're saying is beginning to make sense but I can't get my head round the thought of an all-powerful Being creating someone like, say, Hitler and then organising his extermination of the Jews.

A: The all-powerful Being did not organise the extermination of the Jews but knew that the outcome would be genocide. That outcome was already in place in His mind although it was yet to happen through the free choice of one section of mankind. If we go back to the quantum world, we know the universe comprises balancing opposites like positive/negative, yin/yang, male/female, good/evil etc. Opposites pervade everything and everywhere, from the atom to galaxies, our earth included. So, our cosmic drama is being directed by both good and evil forces, which is something we have no overall control over. But we do have control of our own thoughts and actions, even if the outcome in our earthly dimension is already decided. The important thing is who we become as we play our parts.

Q: I still say you're asking a lot expecting me to swallow all this.

A: It is not easy to accept that all existence is already in place but will not become reality until some form of consciousness, like human thought, gives it form. Like every revolutionary idea in science or philosophy or religion, this hypothesis requires a fundamental shift in consciousness. If we can make that transition it could liberate humanity's imagination to the same degree that, say, Zero Point physics can liberate the energy in so-called empty space. And, talking of Zero Point physics -

This idea that the vacuum of space is really a cauldron of fluctuating energies is in profound accord with the views of nearly all spiritual traditions: that everything is inseparably one, that all that manifests is arising within the same unified ocean of being. There are no separations. All of humanity and in fact the entire universe is one coherent body.

Thought worth pondering: The Big Bang that started

the universe was also a Big Bang of consciousness through which everything, animate and inanimate, is connected.

3 UNDER ATTACK FROM THE MIND VAMPIRES

ELEMENTALS, DEMONS, NEGATIVE ENERGIES, ALLAN KARDEK, POLTERGEISTS, POSSESSION.

We are under attack! Never before in the history of human existence has man's inhumanity to man been more evident. There is a seething, incomprehensible hatred everywhere. People today commit more murders, rapes, atrocities, robberies, acts of terror and hatred than ever before. Some are consumed by selfishness and greed and care not for human, animal or any other form of life. They have plunged the world into a downward spiral of turmoil from which we may never recover.

We are being bombarded by forces surrounding us - advertising, politics, sport, food, drink, sex etc. We respond to these forces almost without thinking. We behave as machines in thrall. Negative forces produce in us anxiety, fear, hatred, greed, lasciviousness, hysteria, stupidity, dullness and boredom. While positive forces, if they are allowed, give us compassion, forbearance, patience, serenity, courage, mercy and pity. The choice is ours which forces we are influenced by.

The Mind Vampires are busily doing their job. And they seem to be winning a spiritual Armageddon. They gather their strength from self-reinforcing negative energies siphoned off the violent Group Soul. As the human race is being infected, some can only watch and wonder.

Why aren't we harnessing those same energies to provide a counter attack of positive vibrations? Because we are sleep walking through our lives, our minds screening out 90 per cent of competing images, sounds, smells, tastes and feelings that are not relevant to our survival. The remaining 10 per cent is a battleground with rival demands clamouring for our attention.

Scientists have said that if we did not learn to shut ourselves off from most of the daily cacophony we would go mad. But, by withdrawing into our mental bunkers we are also denying ourselves powers that are ready, willing and waiting to change our lives. By withdrawing our heads into our shells like tortoises we are playing into the hands of those entities which share our dimension but which are intent on satisfying their own, base motives. We make ourselves helpless in the face of forces around us.

So, what are we going to do to help ourselves and, perhaps at the same time, make the world a better place? Firstly, we must draw on the special gift exclusively bestowed on us humans by the Cosmic Mind and tap into that unlimited reservoir of power 'out there' and all around us. To do this we have to acknowledge and believe in the power of our consciousness and harness our minds to positive energies. Then guard carefully what comes in, making sure we admit only that which is positive, healthful and good.

Thought power can change things and people; it can be either positive or negative. Hostile thought pressure and the essence of a 'curse' are one and the same thing.

Let's look at some different manifestations of what I have named Cosmogenic Energy to see how it exhibits its power while continuing to baffle the most eminent of scientific brains.

The first thing to recognise is that there are discreet energies which exist alongside our own dimension which are also part of our 'resonating soup' of vibrations. It is important that we acknowledge these other energies because it will help us see the whole picture and how the pieces of the cosmic jigsaw fit together and affect our lives.

Spiritual gurus down the ages have contended that we are surrounded by entities that we cannot see but are real in their own dimensions. Since science maintains energy cannot be destroyed, it can only change form, it seems logical that extreme emotions like hate, fear, love etc send out their own vibrations which, like a charge of electricity, find a haven with other, like, energies. So, in our daily lives we feed these energies and entities who can then return to us to help or harm us.

Our world seems to be the natural habitat of negative entities, which defy any known system of reference. Their logic dominates the material world of politics and commerce, in which man's inhumanity to man is a familiar experience -

where tyranny prospers and evil empires flourish.

Lurking out of the visible spectrum are populations of these unseen beings who take the form of whatever the mind desires. They are 'tuning in' to the myriad energies that abound in the universe, including those we humans have created, and they feed on them to sustain their forms. They are active and intelligent and are able to act physically on people in the same way as people act physically on each other.

There are a lot of low spirits abounding in the universes next door awaiting opportunities to partake, second-hand, of the old lusts and thrills of earthly life. Some are activated by malice, others merely mischievous, but they draw their energies from their hosts, or whatever is available in the invisible realm. Low moral ideals (low vibrations) attract these low spirits while high ideals (high vibrations) do the opposite.

Symptoms of Psychic Attacks and Dark Energies

There are many different symptoms that can indicate negative and dark psychic energies, spirits or entities. The following list identifies a few major pointers. But these symptoms can also indicate other types of health problems so it's important to investigate all possibilities.

- Suddenly acting totally out of character

- Major changes in behaviour for no reason

- A loss of memory

- Major changes in clarity of thinking or analytical ability

- Sudden ongoing fatigue for no apparent reason

- A drained feeling

- Icy cold feeling on part or all of your body

- Hearing someone's voice regularly

- Hearing voices generally

- Recurrent or frequent nightmares

- Strange or recurring accidents

- Feeling someone is watching you

- A discomfort or fear in a specific room or area in your home or office

- A drastic loss of self-confidence

- A sudden loss of energy

- Sudden illnesses that elude diagnosis

- Sudden illnesses that cannot be explained

- Feeling someone touch you or bump into you when nobody is present

- Sensing a presence

- Sensing a large pair of eyes watching you or following you

- Sudden or irrational difficulties with finances or relationships

- Imagining monsters, animals or frightening shadows

- Sudden depression without an apparent cause

- Seeming ongoing bad luck

- Visions or hallucinations

- Irrational fear, anger or sorrow

- A negative obsessive thought, desire or fetish that won't go away

The view that we are constantly being influenced by invisible intelligent entities is strongly supported by a Frenchman who gained a great following in the mid to late 1800s. He rejoiced in the name of Hypolyte Leon Denizard Rivail but became better known, and is still revered by some today, as Allan Kardec. He is considered the father of Spiritism and he had a profound impact on the spiritualist movement.

Rivail was a French educator and philosopher, born in Lyon on 3 October 1804. He spoke several languages, and his impressive intellectual background allowed him to teach courses in comparative physiology, astronomy, chemistry and physics in a prestigious scientific school in Paris. For one of his research papers, he was inducted into the Royal Academy of Arras. He organised and taught free courses for the underprivileged.

In 1854, at the age of 50, Rivail heard of the mysterious paranormal phenomena (table turning) that had taken America and Europe by storm. Despite his scepticism, he was convinced by close friends to attend an experimental meeting where he was able to witness such occurrences first-hand. His intellectual curiosity and scientific instincts told him that there had to be a rational explanation for these phenomena. Consequently, he began soon afterward to conduct investigations of his own.

Using the same logical rigor that he had applied to his work in education and science, Rivail set out to understand the phenomena. He submitted questions to different channels (mediums), in different countries. The answers were compared, analysed, and organised for inclusion in *The Spirits' Book*, which was first published in 1857.

To keep his new area of research apart from his writings on education, Rivail - on the advice of spirit instructors - adopted the name Allan Kardec, which he was told had been his name in a previous incarnation. In addition to the publication of various books, he founded the Spiritist Society of Paris and La Revue Spirite, a journal he edited until his death on 31 March 1869.

In his classic, Le Livre des Esprits (The Spirits' Book), he expounded a new theory of human life and destiny. Its content is based on trance communications received through Mlle Celina Bequet, a professional hypnotist.

The book was a blockbusting hit being published in more than 25 editions which are still widely read in South America, Australia and New Zealand. It is, without question or equal, the primary text among Spiritists.

Among the avalanche of information from the Other Side is a dissertation on the influence that discarnate spirits have on living beings. Interestingly, it chimes in with the view that thoughts are put into our heads from which we make our choices.

One actual question and answer session covered this very point:

Q: Do spirits influence our thoughts and our actions?

A: Their influence upon them is greater than you suppose, for it is very often they who direct both.

After hundreds of these sessions Kardec produced a useful summary of spirit communications. He said: 'Spirits exert an incessant action upon the moral world, and even upon the physical world; they act both upon matter and upon thought, and constitute one of the powers of nature, the efficient cause of many classes of phenomena hitherto unexplained or misinterpreted, and of which only the Spiritist theory can give a rational explanation.

'Spirits are incessantly in relation with men. The good spirits try to lead us into the right road, sustain us under the trials of life, and aid us to bear them with courage and resignation; the bad ones tempt us to evil: it is a pleasure for them to see us fall, and to make us like themselves.

'Spirits are attracted by their empathy with the moral quality of the parties by whom they are evoked. Spirits of superior elevation take pleasure in meetings of a serious character, animated by the love of goodness and the sincere desire of instruction and improvement. Their presence repels the spirits of inferior degree who find, on the contrary, free access and freedom of action among persons of frivolous disposition, or brought together by mere curiosity, and wherever evil instincts are to be met with.

'So, far from obtaining from spirits, under such

circumstances, either good advice or useful information, nothing is to be expected from them but trifling, lies, ill-natured tricks, or humbugging…'

Kardec goes on, 'It is easy to distinguish between good and bad spirits. The language of spirits of superior elevation is constantly dignified, noble, characterised by the highest morality, free from every trace of earthly passion; their counsels breathe the purest wisdom, and always have our improvement and the good of mankind for their aim. The communications of spirits of lower degree, on the contrary, are full of discrepancies, and their language is often commonplace, and even coarse. If they sometimes say things that are good and true, they more often make false and absurd statements, prompted by ignorance or malice. They play upon the credulity of those who interrogate them, amusing themselves by flattering their vanity, and fooling them with false hopes.

'They {the higher spirits/thoughts} teach us that selfishness, pride, sensuality, are passions which bring us back towards the animal nature, by attaching us to matter; that he who, in this lower life, detaches himself from matter through contempt of worldly trifles, and through love of the neighbour, brings himself back towards the spiritual nature; that we should all make ourselves useful, according to the means which God has placed in our hands for our trial; that the strong and the powerful owe aid and protection to the weak; and that he who misuses strength and power to oppress his fellow-creature violates the law of God.

'They teach us that, in the spirit-world, nothing can be hidden, and that the hypocrite there will be unmasked, and all his wickedness unveiled; that the presence, unavoidable and perpetual, of those whom we have wronged in the earthly life is one of the punishments that await us in the spirit-world; and that the lower or higher state of spirits gives rise in that other life to sufferings or to enjoyments unknown to us upon the earth.'

The spirits even had a view remarkably similar to Rupert Sheldrake's morphic resonance (of which more later):

Q: Whence comes it that the same idea - that of a discovery, for instance - so often suggests itself at the same time to several persons, although they may be at a distance from one another?

A: When you say that an idea is 'in the air' you employ a figure of speech that is much nearer the truth than suppose. Everyone helps unconsciously to propagate it.

If Kardec's communicators are right, we human beings can plug into either those powers that are positive and use them to fight off evil influences and control our own destinies. Or, let negative energies have their way with us.

Noted US psychologist, Dr Edith Fiore, believed that depression, phobias, addiction and many other disorders among her patients were caused, not by mental illness but by spirits who, after death, remained in the physical world as 'displaced persons' inhabiting the bodies and minds of those still living. Their hosts – Dr Fiore's patients - were unwittingly taking on whatever ailment these 'cuckoos in the nest' had brought with them, including many physical illnesses.

This spirit possession was resistant to orthodox treatment but responded almost miraculously to a benign form of exorcism called Spirit Release. Dr Fiore was so intrigued by her experiences that she wrote a book about them called *The Unquiet Dead*. Another book written 60 years earlier, which has become a classic among those dealing with spirit possession, is *Thirty Years Among The Dead* by Carl Wickland.

Dr Wickland (1861-1945) was a member of the Chicago Medical Society, the American Association for the Advancement of Science, and the chief psychiatrist at the National Psychopathic Institute of Chicago. He specialised in cases of schizophrenia, paranoia, depression, addiction, manic-depression, criminal behaviour and phobias. After moving to Los Angeles in 1918, he founded the National Psychological Institute of Los Angeles with his wife Anna Wickland, who was a trance medium. Wickland treated many patients suffering from mental illness of all kinds, and after many years' experience came to the conclusion that a number of patients he treated had 'attachments.'

By that he meant that spiritual entities had attached themselves to unwitting mortals and were influencing them, often in the worst kind of way - leading them to alcoholism, madness, and occasionally murder. Wickland stated at the time, 'Spirit obsession is a fact - a perversion of a natural law - and is amply demonstrable.' He said that to him it had been proven hundreds of times when he had transferred, temporarily, the supposed insanity or aberration from the victim to a psychic sensitive (his wife) who had been trained for the purpose.

Through conversations with the entity, via his wife, Wickland would ascertain the cause of the psychosis. Having come to the 'spirit obsession' conclusion, Wickland and his wife set up a rescue circle, with Mrs Wickland acting as the medium, and they set about communicating with lost souls who had passed away and were unaware of their post physical death condition and often in denial due to dogmatic religious, or equally dogmatic atheist beliefs.

In the book's introduction the author writes, 'The change called death, the word is a misnomer-universally regarded with gloomy fear, occurs so naturally and simply that the greater number, after passing out of the physical are not aware that the transition has been made, and having no knowledge of a spiritual life they are totally unconscious of having passed into another state of being. Deprived of their physical sense organs, they are shut out from the physical light, and lacking a mental perception of the high purpose of existence, these individuals are spiritually blind and find themselves in a twilight condition - the outer darkness mentioned in the Bible - and linger in the realm known as the Earth sphere.'

The book documents a number of cases of both anonymous and well-known communicators such as Helena Blavatsky; co-founder of the Theosophy movement, and Mary Baker-Eddy, the founder of Christian Science. A number of subjects are discussed including crime, suicide, materialism, selfishness, and narcotics.

Coming more or less up to date is the case of award-winning journalist Hazel Courteney. When she popped into Harrods on April 8 1998 to buy some Easter eggs something happened which changed her life. As she made her way through the turnstile to the bread hall it stuck fast – it wouldn't go forward, it wouldn't go back. As Hazel was deciding her next move...well, let her take up the story in her own words...

'I felt a searing bolt of – of something – coursing through my body. I can only describe it as "energy." The pain in my chest was appalling. I could hear a voice, not my own but inside my head, shouting "See a doctor – now."

That voice, which possibly saved her life, was that of Diana, Princess of Wales who, by that time, had been dead for seven months. Suddenly the turnstile moved and Hazel stumbled towards the exit and found a telephone to call her doctor who, after tests, found no heart problems but diagnosed a severe panic attack. Later that night while lying in bed pondering on the events of the day, the voice returned. It kept repeating, "I have died and come back." Hazel, a perfectly normal and balanced busy wife and mother, had never experienced anything psychic or paranormal. This episode was totally alien to her down-to-earth approach to life. She wrote a book about her experience - *Divine Intervention*.

Possession

This is a more extreme version of 'attachment' where the human psyche is taken over by evil or satanic forces. In the Middle Ages many illnesses, both physical and mental, were said to be due to invading entities. Christian theology then deemed the concept of demonic possession heretical, so anyone displaying unusual behaviour, or a strange personality, was automatically suspected of being possessed by the Devil.

Possession by a demonic entity later became regarded as superstition. But is it? There are plenty of cases today which mirror medieval examples of being demonically possessed, when the victim appears to suffer from a complete behaviour takeover by a demonic entity. In fact the entity may dominate the victim to such an extent that the person it inhabits 'becomes' whatever has taken him over.

Going back in time, an extreme example of demonic possession was the 'Devils of Loudun' case in which, in the 17th Century, an entire convent of French Ursuline nuns began to blaspheme, spit and writhe on the ground as if possessed. Those who tried to exorcise the demons became victims themselves (an example here of forces, this time negative, being transmitted, just as positive energies are apparently exchanged in Subud – more on this later). One died insane, another expired frothing at the mouth and blaspheming and another went mad years later writhing on the ground barking and hissing. A friar kneeling in prayer nearby was infected and he, too, began writhing and hissing.

One of the original investigators, Jesuit Father Jean-Joseph Surin, also succumbed and was horrified that when he tried to make the sign of the cross something would push his hand aside and he would be compelled to bite himself. He wrote later, 'An alien spirit is united to mine, without depriving me of consciousness or inner freedom, and yet constituting a second me as though I had two souls.'

The Catholic Church still defines true signs of possession as displaying superhuman strength, often accompanied by fits and convulsions, changes in personality, having knowledge of the future or other secret information and being able to understand and converse in languages not previously known to the victim.

Arthur Guirdham, a psychiatrist working for the UK's National Health Service, once stated, 'People who insist that possession is an old superstition have never seen a case. Or if they have, have been so blinkered by prejudice that they have temporarily lost the capacity to assess symptoms.' He details examples of possession in which his patients say, 'Something which is not me gets inside me and makes me do these things.'

He rejects the modern, psychiatric alternative of Multiple Personality Disorder (DID), claiming this is just possession, by one or more spirit entities, by another name. He considers psychic influence or spirit possession to be the cause of many kinds of illness, mental and physical, and other conditions such as sleepwalking and addictions. One of the most extraordinary manifestations of Dissociate Identity Disorder is the ability of many personalities to manifest in one physical body. And it isn't just the voices and personalities that change. In case studies physical differences have been recorded like blue eyes changing to green when one personality swaps to another.

Even more astounding is that while one personality will have cancer, another is cancer-free. One may be diabetic while the other is not. How can this be? How can the same body have the ability to make such dramatic physical transformations? If we knew the answer it could be the key to curing diseases or even halt the ravages of time. Could it be that somehow the dominant personality in the body is selecting from a range of quantum probabilities without knowing it?

In her book *Fractals of God* Kathy Forti talks of a client she calls 'Valerie' who was host to 100 personalities. Some were male, some female, there was a 'wild child', some spoke different languages, some were left-handed, some right, some needed glasses, others had perfect eyesight, some had allergies, some not, one was diagnosed as having cancer of the cervix while another was cancer-free.

Another explanation for this weird phenomenon might be

that humans are not only vulnerable to being possessed by one spirit but also perhaps by many. Or, maybe, one spirit can be fractured into many parts. The notion that something of a person's being can be 'transferred' to another is supported by a curiosity arising from some organ transplants. Some recipients notice character traits appearing in themselves that they never had before – for instance a life-long vegetarian will acquire a desire for a juicy steak. Or a lover of pulp fiction will develop a keen appetite for the classics.

The phenomenon is called Cellular Memory Syndrome. Paul Pearsall, a psychoneoroimmunologist, author of *The Heart's Code*, proposes that the cells of living tissue have the ability to remember. He interviewed 150 recipients of heart and other organ transplants. One amazing story he recounts is that of an eight year old girl who received the heart of a girl, aged 10, who had been murdered. After the transplant the recipient had horrifying nightmares of a man murdering her. The dreams were so dramatic that psychiatric help was sought. The girl's images were so specific that the psychiatrist informed the police. He said, 'Using the description from the little girl they found the murderer. The time, weapon, place, the clothes he wore, what the little girl he'd killed had said to him – everything the transplant recipient reported was accurate...'

The connection between spirit possession and Multiple Personality Disorder was brought back into public and professional awareness by psychiatrist Ralph Allison. A chapter in one of his books is entitled, 'Possession and the Spirit World.' In it he describes the effects of spirit interference and the process of releasing the discarnates.

Dr Allison says bluntly that many of his multiple

ANTHONY TALMAGE

personality patients have exhibited symptoms of possession. He described his encounters with aspects of their personalities which were not true alter egos. He found it difficult to dismiss these bizarre occurrences as delusion. With no 'logical' explanation, he has come to believe in the possibility of spirit possession.

He defines five levels or types of possession:

1 Simple obsessive compulsive neurosis

2 Thought forms and created beings

3 An aspect or fragment of the mind of a living person

4 The earthbound spirit who once lived as a human being

5 Full demonic possession

Dr Allison states that he has corresponded with many professionals who have come to similar conclusions about the origin and purpose of alter ego personalities.

Some believe that people can become possessed by toying with the supernatural, using devices like the ouija board and planchettes. I go along with this theory - it's the equivalent of throwing open your front door and yelling, 'Anyone out there's welcome to come in and take what you want.'

Poltergeists

In the strange phenomena associated with poltergeists, for instance, we have an extreme example of unexplained energy, seemingly out of the control of the human who produced it.

The word Poltergeist is the German for noisy ghost. In hundreds of authenticated cases from the 11th to the 21st centuries impossible things happen which no-one has been able to replicate in scientifically-controlled conditions. Somehow, invisible energies start fires, move furniture, hurl stones, write on walls, smash crockery, produce knockings, speak in disembodied voices, play havoc with electrical appliances, and even produced a rainstorm inside a house.

Usually the phenomena is said to be connected with disturbed children, often at the time of puberty. The theory being that, somehow, the emotional turmoil is externalising itself without the knowledge of its source.

One of the most spectacular examples of this 'noisy ghost' activity became known as the Enfield Poltergeist case. Manifestations lasted from August 1977 to September 1978. During this time a mother and her four children, who were living in a council house in Enfield, London, experienced the spectrum of poltergeist phenomena. Over 1500 separate incidents were recorded.

Things started mildly with just a few unexplained sounds and then progressed to alleged possession and other more disturbing occurrences. It seemed as if an intelligence was at work behind the phenomena because it consistently thwarted attempts by investigators to gather meaningful evidence.

In one instance, a toy brick was said to have materialised out of thin air, flew across the room and hit a photographer on the head. But the cameraman was not quick enough to capture any images of the assault. Many items caught fire of their own accord and metal objects bent out of shape.

The worst manifestation was the apparent possession of 12 year old Janet, from whom emitted a deep gruff voice. Janet was also reported to have been constantly levitated out of bed at night by an unseen force, effectively trapping her on the ceiling on occasions.

All in all the Enfield Poltergeist became known as a classic of its kind.

After studying hundreds of cases I have come to the conclusion that the highly-charged psychic energy is actually being hi-jacked by a lower-order entity who uses it to behave rather like a dim-witted hooligan.

Why it does this, and how, are two questions for later. In the meantime, the important fact is that somehow energy given off by a human life is being manipulated to affect the world around us. So, if a person's thoughts, or emotions, can be transmuted to levitate a heavy object, surely the thoughts and emotions of us all are being transmitted all the time to either positive, or negative, effect. And, the reverse happens and this is what is occurring today as an army of marauding negative energies is sweeping across our earthly plane, hi-jacking the human psyche.

The late Muhammad Subuh Sumohadiwidjojo, an Indonesian known as Bapak, founder of the world-wide spiritual movement called Subud, contended that the Cosmic Order comprises five levels, each existing as a world of its own. These levels, he averred, are material, vegetable, animal, human and divine. And each world is full of number-less life forces continually seeking haven within the human heart.

Not long before he died in 1987, Muhammad Subuh

startled his followers by telling them that the world was populated by invisible entities, far greater in number than people. And that these beings were constantly on the lookout for opportunities to bend people to their will. He warned his supporters to be on their guard and not to allow these negative forces into their lives.

Because the subject of Subud comes up later in this book, it is worth spending a few minutes looking at some useful background. Muhammad Subuh had humble beginnings living in a hamlet just outside Semarang in East Java. In 1924 he was an employee of the local municipality and, besides his job, he was studying bookkeeping three evenings a week. It was his habit to take a walk at around midnight to get some air. One such night, just in front of a hospital under construction called the Centrale Burgerlijke Ziekenhuis, a brilliant light in the sky enveloped him. He began shaking and trembling violently and he thought he was having some kind of heart attack.

He was only about 300 metres from where he lived so hurried home and threw himself on his bed. He noticed that the light was now inside his body and he was filled with a radiance. He was then motivated by a supernatural energy to stand and walk about, his body shaking and vibrating. The experience seemed to have a cleansing effect on his life, physically, mentally and spiritually. This phenomenon went on night after night until finally it petered out.

Muhammad Subuh was guided by an inner voice (do we assume that this voice represented one of the universe's 'good guys'?) to pass the energy on. He discovered he could do this if he stood in quiet contemplation while others gathered around him. These people were 'opened' and those who 'received' the energy found they, in turn, could communicate it to others. As one candle will light another, gradually thousands of people around the world received the power.

The word Subud is a contraction of three Sanskrit words: Susila Budhi Dharma. In Subud terminology, these have been interpreted as follows:

Susila means 'right living'; Budhi refers to 'the higher powers and capacities latent in man himself' and Dharma means 'submission to the Will of God'.

Taken together, they mean 'Right living according to the highest that is possible for man in submission to God's will.'

The unique aspect of Subud is that it is not a religion, has no teaching but is regarded as a 'learning experience.' Its members claim to receive the Great Life Force through practising a spiritual exercise known in Indonesian as the latihan kejiwaan, or inner training. This amounts to getting in the right frame of mind, letting go and then allowing the energy to move your body in any way it deems fit.

The Subud movement crosses all racial divides and religious boundaries. Many members claim their religious beliefs have strengthened as a result of meeting twice a week together to submit to the energy in the latihan.

But what is this energy? As thousands the world over would attest to having received some kind of force into their lives, there can be no doubt that the phenomenon is real. To my mind the influence, whatever it is, is just another manifestation (an apparently positive one) of the many energies in the Cosmogenic firmament.

Bapak (the Indonesian word for father) remained humble at heart throughout the rest of his life, insisting that he was nothing special and that the power was a gift from God to cleanse and guide the human heart. In his talks to his followers he would say that man was open to sub-human powers which stimulate him to do evil and violence. These powers, he said, dictated people's conduct as they submitted to this alien influence without realising what was going on. Man's feelings, heart and mind, he said, are permeated by these forces.

Bapak said that in his sea of five dimensions, each a world of its own with its own beings, energies were continuously seeking 'soul mates' with whom to combine. Man's actions are therefore influenced by whatever spirits he invites in. This, Bapak taught, could lead to misery blotting out other, higher forces, and setting up sicknesses in mind and body.

Conversely, he said, we can overcome this contamination by tuning into higher forces which would eject lower orders. This higher power would intervene to the extent of a person's need and capacity to receive. If a person allows the High Life Force to flow into him or her, it would not only be that person's protection but would also flow from them to others and from them to more still until an immense power gathered strength. We look at this experience in greater detail later. Basically, though, for you and me the philosophy can be summed up as...be as positive as possible about our daily life, despite setbacks and challenges. The more positive we are, the more beneficial energies we gather to ourselves and those around us. And, of course, the opposite is the case. The choice is ours.

But Bapak was not alone in being embraced by a 'divine

light.'

At the turn of the 20th century, Canadian psychiatrist Richard Maurice Bucke published an intriguing work entitled Cosmic Consciousness: A Study in the Evolution of the Human Mind. Dr Bucke argued that experiences of 'Illumination,' far from being a symptom of mental instability, were in fact a feature of highly evolved human minds.

Bucke himself had had such an experience, which he described as 'being wrapped around, as it were, by a flame-coloured cloud.' The next instant he knew that the light was within himself. Directly after this came a sense of exultation, of immense joyousness, accompanied or immediately followed by an intellectual illumination almost impossible to describe. Into his brain streamed one momentary lightning flash of Brahmic splendour which has ever since lightened his life.

Bucke went on to interview 50 or so others who he had come across who had had similar experiences. Typically they described their encounters, as: '…the gladness and rapture of love, so intensified that it became an ocean of living, palpitating light, the brightness of which outshone the brightness of the sun…'

Shortly after Bucke's work, psychologist William James published his 'Varieties of Religious Experience.' His patients described their experiences in familiar terms…

'…suddenly, without warning, I felt as if I were in Heaven - an inward state of peace and joy and assurance indescribably intense, accompanied by a sense of being bathed in a warm glow of light…'

'...When (experiences such as this) came, I was living the fullest, strongest, sanest, deepest life... I was aware that I was immersed in the infinite ocean of God...'

So, on the one hand with destructive poltergeists and on the other the inner power bestowed by some apparently divine force, we have two extremes of negative and positive invisible powers working in human lives. As Bapak contended, there are myriad entities out there watching for the opportunity to intervene in human affairs. Here are some of the more commonly accepted manifestations of these energies:

Elementals

Generally known as nature spirits but this is just a way of rationalising a raw energy that seems to have an intelligence of its own - another example of negative emotions manifesting themselves in some physical way. Envy or hatred is produced subconsciously and this is projected outwards and then returns to its creator to dwell in his mind forming negative habits and obsessions.

Demons

Demons are negative energies with a personality that integrates with those of their victims. They are 'invisible beings' with wicked intelligence wandering on our plane seeking living bodies in which they can express themselves. These spirits are personalities and have characteristics that make up an intelligent being. They walk, hear, speak, see, obey, seek, think, know and dwell in the body to accomplish their purposes. They have no other means of influencing our world, other than through our living beings.

Thought forms

In some cultures it is accepted without question that thought can create an entity which seems to have a mind of its own. There are hundreds of examples but one that illustrates the point well is that chronicled by Alexandra David-Neel, one of those extraordinary women of the late 19th and early 20th Century who journeyed alone to live with remote tribes or cultures.

It was in Tibet where she studied the mystical subject of tulpa creation. A tulpa, according to traditional Tibetan doctrines, is an entity created by an act of imagination, rather like the fictional characters of a novelist, except that tulpas are not written down but appear as three-dimensional figures.

David-Neel became so interested in the concept that she decided to try to create one. It is worth quoting verbatim here from her book *Magic and Mystery in Tibet* (University Books 1965):

'However interested we may feel in the other strange accomplishments with which Tibetan adepts of the secret lore are credited, the creation of thought forms seems by far the most puzzling.

'Phantoms, as Tibetans describe them, and those that I have myself seen, do not resemble the apparitions which are said to occur during spiritualist séances.

'As I have said, some apparitions are created on purpose either by a lengthy process...or, in the case of proficient adepts, instantaneously or almost instantaneously. In other cases, apparently the author of the phenomenon generates it unconsciously, and is not even in the least aware of the apparition being seen by others'.

She goes on, 'However, the practice is considered as fraught with danger for everyone who has not reached a high mental and spiritual degree of enlightenment and is not fully aware of the nature of the psychic forces at work in the process.

'Once the tulpa is endowed with enough vitality to be capable of playing the part of a real being, it tends to free itself from its maker's control. This, say Tibetan occultists, happens nearly mechanically, just as the child, when his body is completed and able to live apart, leaves its mother's womb.

'Sometimes the phantom becomes a rebellious son and one hears of uncanny struggles that have taken place between magicians and their creatures, the former being severely hurt or even killed by the latter.

'Tibetan magicians also relate cases in which the tulpa is sent to fulfil a mission, but does not come back and pursues its peregrinations as a half-conscious, dangerously mischievous puppet. The same thing, it is said, may happen when the maker of the tulpa dies before having dissolved it. Yet, as a rule, the phantom either disappears suddenly at the death of the magician or gradually vanishes like a body that perishes for want of food. On the other hand, some tulpas are expressly intended to survive their creator and are specially formed for that purpose.

'Must we credit these strange accounts of rebellious "materialisations" as phantoms which have become real beings, or must we reject them all as mere fantastic tales and wild products of imagination?

'Perhaps the latter course is the wisest. I affirm nothing. I only relate what I have heard from people whom, in other circumstances, I had found trustworthy, but they may have deluded themselves in all sincerity.

'Nevertheless, allowing for a great deal of exaggeration and sensational addition, I could hardly deny the possibility of visualizing and animating a tulpa. Besides having had few opportunities of seeing thought-forms, my habitual incredulity led me to make experiments for myself, and my efforts were attended with some success.'

David-Neel then gives an account of her own attempt to create a tulpa. 'In order to avoid being influenced by the forms of the lamaist deities, which I saw daily around me in paintings and images, I chose for my experiment a most insignificant character: a Monk, short and fat, of an innocent and jolly type.

'I shut myself in tsams and proceeded to perform the prescribed concentration of thought and other rites. After a few months the phantom Monk was formed. His form grew gradually, fixed and lifelike looking. He became a kind of guest, living in my apartment. I then broke my seclusion and started for a tour, with my servants and tents.

'The Monk included himself in the party. Though I lived in the open, riding on horseback for miles each day, the illusion persisted. I saw the fat tulpa; now and then it was not necessary for me to think of him to make him appear. The phantom performed various actions of the kind that are natural to travellers and that I had not commanded. For instance, he walked, stopped, looked around him.

'The illusion was mostly visual, but sometimes I felt as if a robe was lightly rubbing against me, and once a hand seemed to touch my shoulder.

'The features which I had imagined, when building my phantom, gradually underwent a change. The fat, chubby-cheeked fellow grew leaner, his face assumed a vaguely mocking, sly, malignant look. He became more troublesome and bold. In brief, he escaped my control.

'I ought to have let the phenomenon follow its course, Once, a herdsman who brought me a present of butter, saw the tulpa in my tent and took it for a living lama. But the presence of that unwanted companion began to prove trying to my nerves; it turned into a "day-nightmare." Moreover, I was beginning to plan my journey to Lhasa and needed a quiet brain devoid of other preoccupations, so I decided to dissolve the phantom. I succeeded, but only after six months of hard struggle. My mind-creature was tenacious of life.

'There is nothing strange in the fact that I may have created my own hallucination. The interesting point is that in these cases of materialization, others see the thought-forms that have been created.'

David-Neel's story indicates the ability of our thoughts to take on a more permanent form, leave the control of the creator and assume a life and intelligence of their own. And then put up quite a fight to maintain their existence. Another reason, surely, for us to think only kind, positive thoughts?

Negative energies in general

These can appear as negative thoughts, negative actions,

negative speech or conversation, negative emotions giving rise to undesirable affects such as illnesses. Negative energies can linger in the atmosphere and can even, some say, carry over from previous lives having lain dormant for many years.

Emotions like fear, hatred, guilt, anger, jealousy, anxiety, misery, and depression have a powerfully negative impact on the world around us so we should counter the effect by consciously conjuring up positive thoughts and emotions. You'd be surprised what a difference it can make to your daily life.

Q: Are you suggesting, in this Age of space travel and the Internet, that we humans are just the playthings of various entities who take over our minds and bodies to fulfil their own agendas?

A: As I said earlier, the Cosmic Drama is unfolding as we think our thoughts and make our decisions. But our minds are a battleground in which positive and negative energies are vying for supremacy. When we decide to mug an old lady instead of help her across the street it is a victory for the Lower Orders.

Q: You've given examples of 'good' energies like that supposedly received in Subud and 'bad' energies that take a person over when they are possessed - aren't these just extremes and most of us live our lives out in the neutral area in between?

A: Not so. These extremes as you call them are more and more becoming the norm. I believe that because of modern communications like social media the power of negative thought energy is increasing all the time and feeding off itself.

Q: Even so, most of us seem to live fairly humdrum lives without any need to murder or rape or steal.

A: Which means that positive energies are also having their effect. However, those positive energies are under siege and could do with some reinforcement.

Q: Using good old fashioned terms, it does seem from what you say that evil forces outnumber good forces. Is this how you see it?

A: I prefer to think of it in terms of negative and positive. I believe that negative forces are finding fertile ground in our 21st Century. But I also believe that positive energies are all around us too and if we have a greater 'energy awareness' more people would produce positive thoughts and this would negate the effects of what I have called The Mind Vampires.

Q: You say that thoughts have the power to actually create physical effects, can you give me an example?

A: Thoughts are translating into physical effects around us all the time. We can see it in the daily acts of violence and aggression in our streets and cities. And now with the advent of Islamist movements like the so-called Islamic State we can see pure evil manifest. But I guess you mean thought power acting on physical objects as in psycho-kinesis. Well, that of course is what happens in poltergeist phenomena. But a couple of people who have demonstrated PK abilities were Stanislawa Tomczyk and Nina Kulagina. Polish-born Tomczyk could levitate small objects and, in 1910, she was tested by a group of scientists at the Physical Laboratory in Warsaw where she produced remarkable physical phenomena under strict test conditions.

Russian Nina Kulagina demonstrated her powers by mentally moving a wide range of objects, including matches, bread, large crystal bowls, clock pendulums, a cigar tube and a salt shaker.

Thought worth pondering: The laws of the universe are only suggestions

4 THE ENERGY AT WORK

COLLECTIVE UNCONSCIOUS, MORPHIC RESONANCE, AKASHIC RECORD, MATHEMATICAL PRODIGIES, PLANT AWARENESS, CLAIRVOYANCE, SYNCHRONICITY, LUCK, LEVITATION, MIRACLES, PRECOGNITION (ANIMAL & HUMAN) HEALING, TELEKINESIS, DOWSING, REINCARNATION, PSYCHOMETRY.

There is a power outside of ourselves which is constantly being tapped into by us, but most of the time we are unaware of it. Thoughts come into our heads and we act on them like robots.

Besides the detrimental environment that can be caused by what dowsers call geopathic stress, there are other 'bad energies' that can infect our space and therefore us.

The material world around us that we can see and touch

and with which we interact, is just the visible surface of a seething flux of energies which govern our lives. We can't see them but we interact, consciously or unconsciously, every moment of our earthly lives. These unseen swirlings can perform feats which are undeniable but which no-one can explain.

For instance, as already mentioned, poltergeists – those noise infestations that move the furniture about or make objects disappear, people float in mid-air, solid things pass through walls and other impossible things. How does this energy manifest itself? How does it perform seemingly impossible feats? And what is the intelligence behind it? Experts now believe that 'something' sucks the energies from human beings and uses these energies for its own purposes. And there you have just another kind of 'bad energy' that could be infesting your home or office.

But these 'bad energies' need not be as dramatic as a poltergeist. They can be negative thought forms from you or anyone else who has been in your home or office. Or they can be negative emotions imprinted on one location which just hang around infecting people's moods or demeanour. They can be traumatised or displaced spirits or non-human entities or energy from curses or psychic attack. All these resonancies hang around making life difficult in one way or another. So, they need to be cleared out and the remaining environment rebalanced and cleansed. How? See the section on dowsing later in this book.

It is worth re-emphasising that thoughts have power. If this was not the case why have people down the centuries prayed to their own personal gods for help? Prayer + Emotion is thought with the focus of a laser beam. So, as we have already said, beware of negative thoughts which carry enough energy to add to the pain of Mother Earth. Loving thoughts, on the other hand, repel negativity. They can do magic. So, be one of Gaia's good guys and broadcast positive vibrations as much as you can.

There are some in the world who are already focused on achieving change and this potent desire is transmitted like a radio signal through the Cosmogenic Field. As like attracts like, the thoughts gather force and start a revolution going.

On the negative side this is what is happening in the modern phenomenon of terrorism. The rise of ISIS is just one result. Belief + Desire + Visualisation + Emotion equals a powerful psychic force pulsing around the globe. With the aid of modern communications the force is magnified until a conflagration starts.

But those who oppose chaos have equal powers to help neutralise the work of the fanatic. There is something out there willing and waiting to alter and widen our individual influence on life around us. It is waiting for us to wake up and start co-operating. Our minds are the link and they contain a facility that can change things. Think angels and there will angels be.

British biologist Dr Rupert Sheldrake contends that the form, development and behaviour of all living organisms are moulded by a field of energy, which behaves as if controlled by a universal consciousness. This superintelligence, he suggests, creates invisible 'templates' which are then modified along the way by changes and developments 'learned' by each species.

Thus, developing embryos 'tune into' the template of

members of the same species to grow into what is expected of them. An acorn becomes an oak tree, tadpoles become frogs, human sperm becomes a baby. Along the way, says Sheldrake, new behaviour patterns are absorbed by the templates as the species evolve.

Sheldrake calls the templates 'morphic fields' and the method of transmission 'morphic resonance,' both of which operate independently of space and time. He wraps up all these controversial ideas under a general hypothesis which he calls Formative Causation.

He suggests that human societies are governed by social and cultural morphic fields, which embrace and organise all that live within them. He says that although comprised of thousands and thousands of individual human beings, a society can function and respond as a unified whole via the characteristics of its morphic field. As examples of similar fields he points to a magnetic field, which is both within a magnet and around it, and a gravitational field, which is both within the earth and around it. Thus field theories take us beyond the traditional rigid definition of 'inside' and 'outside.'

So, here we have the first building block to support the idea that the universe is a swirling mass of influences which envelope us all.

How do cuckoos manage to 'clone' the eggs in their host nest producing the exact colouring and speckled spots of those in there already? How do homing pigeons find their way to their loft from hundreds or even thousands of miles away?

I believe it is allied to Sheldrake's theory. When the cuckoo settles on the nest to leave an alien egg some mechanism in the bird reproduces the exact frequencies (wave form in quantum physics) that makes up the physical egg and, like a 3-D photocopier, reproduces the same colouring and texture – enough to fool the host bird.

Similarly, a pigeon's base location comprises a unique melange of frequencies which the bird has absorbed into itself while 'acclimatising' to its home. Once released hundreds of miles away the base frequency 'calls' to its twin frequencies within the bird and the pigeon homes in on the direction. This is similar to a dowser finding the direction of an underground water supply, even when it's on a map.

The common denominator is the package of unique frequencies in both the transmitter and the receiver which are connected by the phenomenon of quantum entanglement.

Sheldrake's theory is not just a crazy shot in the dark by a maverick scientist out to make a name for himself with some outlandish new idea. His hypothesis is a development of Swiss psychologist Carl Jung's theory of the Collective Unconscious, in which he posits that all mankind contributes to, and can access, a 'sea' of thought, emotion and information and when we die we are absorbed into this super-consciousness. Sheldrake takes this further by suggesting that a similar principle operates throughout ALL life in the universe, not just in human beings.

Sheldrake and Jung represent two eminent minds concluding that a vast, primordial energy-field of thoughts, ideas, information, emotion and feelings is swirling around 'out there.' This maelstrom is surging in and out of human affairs imposing a divine order on some things and creating a demonic madness on others.

Floating about in it all, and as all-pervading as the air we breathe, are thoughts. And this would explain why discoveries are often made simultaneously by different people in different parts of the world inspired, perhaps, by a cosmic will.

Although these theories are discussed here in a relatively modern context, the idea of some kind of universal consciousness is not new. The notion has been passed down through the ages from one civilisation to another. Typical is the so-called Akashic records, believed in by Buddhists, occultists and adherents of the Theosophy religion, who claim that data on everything that has ever happened, is happening or will happen is imprinted on the basic structure of the entire universe.

The 'Akasha' or 'Astral Light' is believed by Theosophists to contain records that persons such as clairvoyants or spiritual beings can tap into. They do this by using their 'astral bodies' or 'astral senses' to gain access to these stored spiritual insights. Someone who probably tapped into the Akashic Record and, as a result, became the best-known psychic in the world was American mystic Edgar Cayce who died in 1945. He was known as the 'sleeping prophet,' the 'father of holistic medicine,' and he was the most documented psychic of the 20th century. Cayce was born on a farm in Hopkinsville, Kentucky, in 1877, and his psychic abilities began to appear as early as his childhood.

As an adult, Cayce would put himself into a state of meditation, connect with the universal consciousness, and from this state came his 'readings'. From holistic health and the treatment of illness to dream interpretation and reincarnation, Cayce's readings and insights offered practical help and advice to thousands of individuals from all walks of life. When 'patients' went to his consulting room Cayce would lie on his couch and go to sleep. While apparently unconscious he would dictate his diagnosis, sometimes using medical terms he had no knowledge of in his waking state. His patients were often completely cured.

English writer Samuel Butler proposed that there is an inherent unconscious memory in all life which dictates instinct, habit, behaviour and even the development of embryos. He took this idea further by suggesting that there is also an inherent memory in atoms, molecules and crystals. I would go further and suggest that all the building blocks of life also contain seeds of their own futures which would explain the 'time slip' phenomena in which people glimpse scenes that have not yet happened.

And Sheldrake's theories continue to evoke controversy. He tells his critics, 'If the kind of radical paradigm shift I am talking about goes on within biology, if the hypothesis of morphic resonance is even approximately correct, then Jung's idea of the collective unconscious would become a mainstream idea.'

Anyone reading these words would be forgiven for giving a sceptical snort. A mysterious medium containing a swirling mass of data communicated across time and space by some indefinable transmission system. Material for a science fiction novel but a belief to steer your life by? Not for anyone who is half-way sane you could say. First of all, where's the proof? A theory is all very well but does it actually have any affect on our lives?

Well, yes it does appear to.

Remember there are two complementary components which make up the theory. Modern technology has presented us with ideal analogies to explain them. Component one: a vast 'supercomputer' in the sky containing all knowledge and component two: a transmitting and receiving station that is continually processing this knowledge. Later in this book we will consider the idea that the brain is not the instigator of thoughts but, rather, a kind of computer processor that handles data pouring in from 'out there.'

First of all though, let's look at the celestial transmission system - Sheldrake's morphic resonance or my Cosmogenic Energy. Somehow this carries thoughts, feelings, images, information and influences of all kinds, with no time lag no matter what the distance, from one place to another.

Supporting the idea that knowledge, information, data or whatever is transmitted into the ether and 'picked up' by receivers, Sheldrake has conducted, or witnessed, numerous experiments that seem to indicate thought power influencing the world around it.

In his book *A New Science of Life* he describes a series of experiments extending over a period of 50 years which proved that, in some inexplicable way, rats seemed to be able to pass on newly-acquired knowledge to other rats around the world. And these were rats of all breeds, not just those descended from trained parents. This legislates against the proposition that knowledge is somehow absorbed into an animal's genes and passed on down the line (more on this theory later).

A similar example of 'learning by telepathy' is quoted by naturalist Lyall Watson who tells of a colony of macaque monkeys, isolated on Koshima Island off the Japanese coast.

They were being observed by primatologists who tempted them nearer by regularly dumping sweet potatoes on the sand. Gradually, a young female learned to make the deliveries more palatable by washing the grit off in the sea. Then, by handing down the trick on a one-to-one basis, the entire colony started to do the same.

Nothing   particularly astonishing in this, perhaps. However, the scientists were amazed to note that, suddenly, ALL colonies of monkeys, isolated on neighbouring islands, were doing the same thing, as if the skill had been plucked out of the air.

In the same extraordinary manner the ability to peck open the old-fashioned foil tops of milk bottles to get at the cream spread at an inexplicable pace among blue tits and great tits. The birds were first observed doing this in Southampton, England, in 1921. Within 20 years the habit had spread across the UK and Europe, but not by heredity as tits tend to stay within a radius of five miles of their normal territory.

Observers who mapped this spreading habit came to the conclusion that the trick must have been independently 'invented' at least 50 times.

Sheldrake proposes that this example demonstrates the evolutionary spread of a new habit not by genetics but through a kind of collective memory, disseminated and absorbed via his Formative Causation.

A detailed study of animal behaviour reinforced his conviction that however invisible and intangible his morphic resonance might be, there was no other explanation for the unexplained powers of animal telepathy, sense of direction and premonitions. In his book, *Dogs That Know When Their Owners Are Coming Home*, he points out that there are millions of animal owners world-wide who will testify to the seemingly magical powers of their dogs, cats, horses, pigeons and parrots. Indeed, of animals, birds and insects of all kinds.

He researched hundreds of cases. But, to ensure he could not be accused of accepting mere anecdotal evidence, he followed a strictly scientific approach in experiments with Jaytee, a male mongrel terrier owned by Pam Smart. Her parents noted that Jaytee seemed to know when Pam was coming home from work and would sit at the French windows in anticipation.

Sheldrake carried out an extensive series of videotaped experiments covering 100 of Pam's absences using different distances, times of day and locations. They showed overwhelmingly that Jaytee seemed to know the moment when Pam *formed the intention* to return home.

Somehow, he was reading her mind, or picking up her thoughts, as they were being formed.

And it would seem that our thoughts can even be felt by plants. In 1966 ex-CIA employee Cleve Backster hooked up house plants to a lie detector and was amazed to note that they seemed to react with 'alarm' when he formed thoughts to harm them. When he decided to burn a leaf of a Draecaena, the plant reacted instantly with the needle of the polygraph jerking wildly. He concluded after many experiments that, somehow, the plants were reading his mind. This fits in with the concept of a mind 'transmitting' negative resonances and affecting the world around it.

An example of thought being absorbed and spreading on the human front might be the growth of National Socialism in Germany in the 1930s when seemingly normal people became infected with a fanaticism that culminated in the attempted extermination of the Jewish race. Unlike the 'innocent' learning element involved in the monkey and blue tit examples, the human version also carried with it a dimension of wickedness, not dissimilar to what is happening today in the realms of so-called Islamic State and international terrorism.

My contention is that this inaudible symphony of data permeating our universe contains powers and forces that influence us on a daily basis with the potential to make us super-human or sub-human, depending on the choices we make. As I have said, I call this swirling mass of influences Cosmogenic Energy. Some physicists have arrived at more or less the same conclusion and they call it the already-mentioned Zero Point Field, more of which later.

So, knowledge is everywhere, all around us in every fragment of time and space. It is easier to picture it as being transmitted like a radio wave but science is now leaning more towards the idea that it simply 'is.' Knowledge just arises in our minds. In his essay on fate Ralph Waldo Emerson said, 'I believe the mind is the creator of the world and is ever creating. Thoughts rule the world.'

Having reached the conclusion that we humans exist in a universe of swirling energies, which are accessible if we use the right methods and have the right attitude (more later) let's look at some of the indicators of those energies.

Weird manifestations

How we are all affected by the energies around us, and how we might manipulate these energies to our own advantage, are exemplified in the wonderful (and some might say wacky) world of Peter and May Belt who run PWB Electronics in Leeds, Yorkshire, UK.

After 30 years manufacturing moving coil loudspeakers, electrostatic loudspeakers, orthodynamic loudspeakers, moving coil headphones and many other audio accessories to aid the listening experience of music lovers, Peter May had a Serendipity Experience which led to a new side to his business. For years Peter had noticed that different factors, not connected with the electronics, were affecting the sound quality of the hi-fi devices. He began experimenting to see if he could pin down a logical cause.

May takes up the story: 'During one set of listening experiments, we had a short coffee break. In the listening room was a small wooden table which had had something spilt on it, causing a nasty stain. Peter decided to treat this stain and applied a chemical to it. No success - the stain was just as bad.

'After the short coffee break we returned to the listening tests. The sound was absolutely appalling! Peter tried everything he knew but could not get the previous 'good' sound back. He knew that the only thing he had done in the past half hour was to apply a chemical to the stain on the small table. He took the table out of the room and listened again. The 'good' sound was back! But with the table returned to the room, the sound was dreadful again. So the table was banished to the garage.'

That episode piqued the couple's interest and started them on a voyage of discovery which changed their lives. May explained that months later she read about a plant under stress that had produced a chemical which was the same as the one they had applied to the stain. Peter wondered if a stress chemical had its opposite – a 'friendly' one. They experimented with every substance they could find until they stumbled on 'chemical X.' After applying it, not to the innards of the electronics but just to the case, the sound was even better than anything they'd heard before.

'Peter then began to wonder that if applying chemical X to a small table could 'improve' the sound. And what would happen if we applied it to other objects in the room - such as a piano, a central heating radiator, wall lights, windows etc. We did this and ended up with the best sound we had ever had!!'

And the rest, as they say, is history. Peter and May Belt began making 'devices' designed to balance energies in the room and improve sound quality. The pair came in for an avalanche of criticism from hi-fi aficionados but there were a few commentators who stuck their heads above the parapet and claimed the devices, against all logic, actually WORKED.

Peter and May stuck to their guns and even offered potential customers free tips on how to improve the sound from their machines. These included placing a plain piece of paper under one of four feet, or pinning back the corner of one curtain in the room, or putting a piece of blue paper under any vase of flowers in the room, or even tying a reef knot in the power cables. All of these ideas have one thing in common – they change the dynamics of the environment. Neither understands WHY this effect happens, only that it does. Could it be nothing to to do with the inherent qualities of the 'additives' and everything to do with the couple's mental *intention* that causes the change?

An experiment that dramatically demonstrate the principles behind their discovery is the Great Freezer Wheeze. They suggest getting two identical CDs and play both noting the quality of the sound. Then, they say, put one CD in the freezer over night. After allowing this to return to room temperature very slowly, play the two CDs again – the frozen one will have taken on an enhanced quality to the other.

The couple have kept details of their discovery, and the ingredients of their products, a closely-guarded secret but they do admit to a strong belief in Rupert Sheldrake's theory of morphic resonance.

Miracles

These are generally regarded as an act of God or Higher Being intervening to prevent or reverse a calamity that is beyond human power to avoid.

If a person who has an incurable disease feels that a divine power is acting in them and the disease is cured, either slowly or quickly, they might say that this cure has been effected by a supernatural force.

In the Christian Bible, miracles are almost commonplace. They fall into six categories:

1 Supernatural acts of creation

2 A temporary and localized suspension of laws regulating nature. Jesus calmed a ferocious storm on the Sea of Galilee

(Matthew 8.23-27), and, on another occasion, He walked upon the waters of the lake (John 6.16-21).

3 Healing - the blind were made to see (John 9.1-7), and the lame to walk (Acts 3.1-10).

4 Power over death. Lazarus, dead four days, was raised (John 11.43-44), and the resurrection of Christ Himself is the very foundation of the Christian belief (1 Corinthians 15.16-19).

5 Expulsion of demons from human bodies (Matthew 12.22). This was evidence of the fact that the Saviour's power was superior to that of Satan.

4 Manipulation of physical things. Christ turned water into wine (John 2.1-11), and multiplied a boy's loaves and fishes, so that thousands were fed (John 6.1-14).

What about miracles since Biblical times?

Divine events, contravening natural laws, have been witnessed by thousands of people at places like Lourdes, Fatima and Medugorje. Thousands who are 'cured' by faith healers will attest to the reality of the modern miracle. Nearly always, the power of belief plays a vital part in enabling miracles to happen.

Precognition

Precognition is the direct knowledge or perception of the future, obtained through extrasensory means. Precognition is the most frequently reported of all extrasensory perception (ESP) experiences, occurring most often (60 to 70 per cent) in dreams. It may also occur spontaneously in waking visions, auditory hallucinations, flashing thoughts entering the mind, and the sense of 'knowing.' Precognitive knowledge also may be induced through trance, channelling, mediumship, and divination.

Usually the majority of precognitive experiences happen within a 48 hour period prior to the future event; most often it is within 24 hours. In rare cases precognitive experiences occur months or even years before the actual event takes place.

Severe emotional shock seems to be a major factor in precognition. By a ratio of 4-1, most concern unhappy events, such as death and dying, illness, accidents, and natural disasters. Intimacy is also a major factor with 80 to 85 per cent of such experiences involving a spouse, family member or friend with whom the individual has close emotional ties. The remainder involves casual acquaintances and strangers, most of whom are victims in major disasters such as aircraft crashes, terrorism outrages or earthquakes.

Psychical researchers estimate that one-third to one-half of all precognitive experiences may provide useful information to avert disasters.

This apparent ability to alter the perceived future is borne out in quantum physics. The most popular theory holds that precognition is a glimpse of a possible future that is based upon present conditions and existing information, and which may be altered depending on acts of free will. That theory implies the future can cause the past, a phenomenon called 'backward causality' or 'retro-causality.'

The Princeton Engineering Anomalies Research (PEAR) group in the US conducted a series of such independent studies which demonstrated the reality of precognition.

Robert Jahn established PEAR in 1979 when he was the Dean of the School of Engineering and Applied Science at Princeton University.   Since that time, this group has been working to better understand 'the role of consciousness in the establishment of physical reality.'   Their results confirm that 30 years ago many of the phenomena that were referred to as 'anomalies' are a normal part of the way the universe operates.

Thousands of experiments proved linkage between the human consciousness and life events. They even proved that thought can influence something that happened in the past! In a random number experiment, based on the heads/tails toss of a coin principle, research physicist Helmut Schmidt discovered his experimenters' thoughts were changing the random patterns days after the patterns had been recorded. In many random number experiments they recorded the number of 'yes's' and 'no's' achieved and, days later, asked assistants to try to influence the bias. Astonishingly, time and again, thought power seemed to reach back through time to have an effect.

In other words, thoughts and intentions have the power to influence both the past and the future. We can extrapolate from this affirmation of our earlier extraordinary conclusion: that the future already exists but that we humans are helping to bring it into being in the same way as we do with a quantum entity by the act of observing.

PEAR concluded that consciousness has capabilities far greater than previously imagined.   Science has now shown this capability and is very uncertain about how to proceed.   In *Science of the Subjective* PEAR's Robert Jahn and Brenda Dunne, say, 'It is not unfounded, therefore, to hope that the same exquisite consciousness that has so brilliantly conceived and refined its science of the objective and that has, at the same time, so fully experienced and celebrated the subjective dimensions of its life, can now finally integrate these complementary perspectives into a super-science of the whole, wherein consciousness will stand as full partner with its cosmos in the establishment of reality.' In other words we could become at one with the Cosmic Mind.

Dowsing

The word 'dowsing' falls far short of encapsulating the mind-boggling possibilities which it offers. I believe that dowsing, or divining, forms a bridge between us and all those swirling energies and information we've been talking about. Anyone can dowse. It's a practical way to access the mysteries of the universe. I've tried to find other, more appropriate words but there just aren't any.

It's a bit like we still use the term 'broadcasting' to describe sending a radio signal from transmitter to receiver. But the word doesn't distinguish between the ordinary and the extraordinary. It could mean anything from a crude walkie-talkie with a range of 10 metres to a satellite 24,000 miles above our heads transmitting a high definition, three dimensional, colour television picture to a 70 inch LED flat screen TV.

In computer terms, dowsing is a kind of spiritual search engine – scanning the ether for answers to anything and everything: From, 'Will this melon be ripe in time for my dinner party on Wednesday?' To, 'How many past lives have I lived?' From, 'Should I wear a waterproof coat today?' To, 'Why is my relationship not working?'

Any of the following words could justifiably be used in connection with aspects of this ancient art...mysterious, supernatural, paranormal, mystical, psychic, clairvoyant, uncanny, bizarre, mumbo-jumbo, weird. Dowsing creates a bridge between two worlds – those of the visible and the invisible. In short, it harnesses the ability still there deep down in each one of us – our intuition. And through honing our intuition, we become increasingly psychic.

And, surprisingly, the basic tools to get started are probably in your own home now and can be adapted at no cost, except for your time.

I'm talking about fashioning sensitive 'L' rods, essential for detecting invisible energies, out of a wire coat hanger. And a weight on the end of a piece of string, cord, twine or chain becomes a pendulum.

The 'L' rod will guide you to the source of any frequency given off by any target, ranging from underground water to earthbound spirits! The pendulum will accurately answer questions with a 'yes', 'no', 'true' or 'false' response. And you can broaden the range of questions using special charts.

Dowsing is like that theoretical wormhole in space that connects far away places - it enables us to jump straight there without the tedious business of travelling thousands of light years and waiting several lifetimes. Dowsing connects us to that 'information field' – which we earlier mentioned as the Akashic Record - which contains everything we will ever need to know.

Here's just one example of how dowsing has produced amazing results:

In 1991, when her daughter's rare, hand-carved harp was stolen, Associate Professor Elizabeth Lloyd Mayer, clinical supervisor at the University of California, Berkeley's Psychology Clinic, did something extraordinary for a dyed-in-the-wool scientific thinker. After the police failed to turn up any leads, a friend suggested she call a dowser, who specialised in finding lost objects.

With nothing to lose—and almost as a joke—Dr. Mayer agreed. Within two days, and without leaving his Arkansas home 1500 miles away, the dowser used a map to locate the exact California street coordinates where the harp was found. This turned Dr Mayer's familiar world of science and rational thinking upside down.

Deeply shaken, yet driven to understand what had happened, Dr Mayer began a fourteen-year journey of discovery which ended in her writing her bestseller *Extraordinary Knowing* that explores what science has to say about this episode and countless other 'inexplicable' phenomena, all of which is routinely familiar to the world of dowsers and psychics where the mind seems to trump the laws of nature.

Among the many abilities the skilled dowser has is one related to clearing those negative energies in the environment we were talking about earlier. In fact some dowsers specialise in transmuting these energies from bad to good for a living. Having detected the location of the bad energies, which can be lines or spirals, their methods vary.

Some use a form of 'earth acupuncture' – banging copper rods into the ground to redirect the lines – while others choose to whirl a pendulum 'unwinding' the energies from their locations. Whatever their chosen method, the dowsers all use one facility in common – their mental INTENT. Yes, there it is again, it's our unconscious minds that are utilised to affect the world around us. There's a comprehensive look at the art of dowsing in my book *Dowse Your Way To Psychic Power* which is available on Amazon outlets worldwide.

The tools for dowsing are rods, pendulums, bobbers and the device everyone recognises – the forked stick. The rods, traditionally known in the US as 'wishing rods', are formed into an L shape and are usually made of copper. The forked stick can be cut from hazel branches or apple, beech or alder. One rod is held in each hand and they swing and cross when the 'target' has been found.

When using a pendulum people might weight the line with a crystal, or other heavy object. Dowsing legend, the late Tom Lethbridge, claimed the important thing seemed to be the length of the line which the pendulum swings on. In his book, *The Power of The Pendulum*, he explains his own experiments into pendulum lengths and also his own theories as to how dowsing works (there's more on the phenomenon of dowsing in Appendix 1). What does seem to be a particular mystery is how diviners can dowse over a map to find people or substances when the focus of the search can be, in some cases, thousands of kilometres away.

Some people earn money by advising mining companies before they carry out test drilling.

Dowsing can be used to detect the subtle energy field surrounding objects, plants, animals, and people. And in energy healing, the diviner dowses the body of a patient before and after treatment, and observes any energy changes.

Dowsers claim that the mind is interacting with the energy field of the object and therefore, they say, it is necessary to be precise about exactly what you are seeking and why, because the rod or pendulum will measure exactly what it's told to. Dowsers constantly remind themselves that *'for results that are terrific it pays to be specific.'* The relationship between Dowsers and Quantum Physics is dealt with in Appendix 1 The Quantum Connection.

Psychometry

This is again sensing the energy of matter - this time by reading objects by touch. Psychometry generally refers to the ability to gain impressions and information about an object, or anything connected to it, by holding it in your hand. A person with this ability is called a Psychometrist or a Scryer.

The term was coined in 1842 by Joseph R. Buchanan, an American physiologist, who claimed it could be used to measure the 'soul' of all things. Buchanan further said that the past is entombed in the present.

Buchanan experimented with some students from Cincinnati Medical School and found that when certain of them where given an unmarked bottle of medicine to handle they had the same reaction as if they had taken the medicine. Buchanan developed the theory that all things give off an 'emanation' (to us this would equate to a unique frequency).

These emanations contained a sort of record of the history of the object. Buchanan believed that objects and places recorded senses and emotions and these could be 'played back' in the mind of the psychometrist.

Some theosophists attempt to explain psychometry in terms of the Akashic records. Psychometrists usually scry in a normal state of mind. In other words there is no preparation needed or any need for an altered state. Scryers are sometimes so sensitive that they may acquire the symptoms of an illness suffered by the owner of an object being held. Psychometric impressions may come in the form of emotions, sounds, scents, tastes or images.

Psychometrists usually experience a loss of energy and an increase in body temperature when scrying. Some scryers report an irregular heartbeat.

It is generally thought that psychometry is a natural power of the human mind, but some people believe that it is controlled by spiritual beings. Some scryers feel that they act as an instrument and that these beings do the actual scrying.

As all objects carry a frequency signature, what psychometrists seem to be doing is connecting with the frequencies of the object in question. This in itself could be said to be a form of clairvoyance.

Rosemary Ellen Guiley in Harper's *Encyclopedia of Mystical & Paranormal Experience*, writes that psychics claim the information is conveyed to them 'through vibrations imbued into the objects by emotions and actions in the past.'

These vibrations are not just some New Age concept, they have a scientific basis as well.

In his book *The Holographic Universe*, Michael Talbot says that psychometric abilities 'suggest that the past is not lost, but still exists in some form accessible to human perception.'

We now know that, on a subatomic level, all matter exists essentially as vibrations and Talbot asserts that consciousness and reality exist in a kind of hologram that contains a record of the past, present and future and psychometrists may be able to tap into that record. In his book *The Psychic Investigator's Casebook* Archibald Lawrie contends that psychics don't tune into past events that have somehow been recorded by the object, or fabric of a building.

Rather, he believes that the object is just a link with the information which is recorded in the cosmic information field. When the psychometrist tunes into the stone or stick or nail s/he is mentally transported to an invisible database of information unlocked by the unique frequency of the object. In other words the object acts as a transceiver connecting the sensitive to the Akashic Record (more on the Akashic Record later).

Reincarnation

There are so many documented cases of past life memories that it would be impractical to list them all. Below is a selection of cases which are impossible to explain with current knowledge.

There are now many recorded examples where under hypnosis a subject has not only recounted details from what appears to be a previous life, but also has spoken a foreign language of which they claim to have had little or no previous knowledge.

A notable case of this is the late actor Glenn Ford. Under hypnosis, he recalled five previous lives - one in particular as a French cavalryman under Louis XIV. The astonishing part was that though Ford said he knew only a few basic phrases in French, under hypnosis he spoke French with ease while describing this life. And when recordings of his regression were sent to UCLA (University of California), they discovered that not only was Ford speaking fluent French, he was in fact speaking the Parisian dialect from the 17th Century.

Jane Evans, a Welsh housewife, agreed to be filmed for BBC television being regressed back to a past life by Arnell Bloxham, president of the British Society of Hypnotherapists and a respected practitioner. She had originally consulted him about rheumatism and, under hypnosis, had revealed seven past lives including one - where the regression was televised - where she identified herself as a Jewish woman living in the city of York in 12th Century England.

She described many details of Jewish life at the time and how she and the local Jews were forced to wear badges to identify themselves. She also spoke of a terrible massacre of the Jewish population by the local townspeople. During this event, she recalled taking shelter with her children in the crypt of a local church, but they were discovered by the mob and that is where she died.

The details were checked by Professor Barrie Dobson, an expert on Jewish history at York University, and he found that her description of 12th Century Jewish life was impressive with its accuracy and in fact he was convinced that some of the details would have only been known to professional historians.

Not only did her regression bring forth obscure details which were historically accurate, it also yielded historical information which should not have been available at that time.

The area of children's past lives is quite remarkable - especially in western countries, where children are rarely exposed to the concept of reincarnation.

Dr Ian Stevenson, Director of Personality Studies at the University of Virginia, devoted 40 years of his professional life to the scientific documentation of past life memories (without hypnosis) of children from all over the world - and has over 3,000 cases in his files.

The Children's Past Lives web site - cases, stories, research, and discussions describe how young children spontaneously remember previous existencies.

Some people have seemingly irrational fears from a young age about such things as drowning, aircraft crashing, loud noises, etc. Often when trying to work through this problem under hypnosis, the person will state that the cause of their phobia is an event from a time when they were someone else - and often the event is the cause of their death in that life.

All Hindus believe that the individual soul exists in a cycle of birth into a body, followed by death and then rebirth. The quality of the next life depends on the soul's Karma - the goodness or badness of their deeds in this life.

A theory about so-called past lives that is gaining ground is that when we enter an altered state we do not access our own past life but merely the frequency of a life that has existed. We pick up the energy field of that life and harmonise our own frequency until the two combine. Hey Presto! We assume the personality of what was a living being and have instant access to its thoughts, memories and character. And some take this a step further believing that this personality hi-jacking is not limited to regression sessions or deep meditation but happens randomly in every day life – a sort of spirit possession.

Levitation

Levitation is a phenomenon of psychokinesis in which objects, people, and animals are lifted into the air without any visibly physical means and float or fly about. The phenomenon has been said to have occurred in mediumship, shamanism, trances, mystical rapture, and demonic possession. Some cases of levitation appear to be spontaneous, while spiritual or magical adepts are said to be able to control it consciously.

There seem to be several general characteristics about levitation. The duration of the phenomenon may last from a few minutes to hours. Generally it requires a great amount of concentration or being in a state of trance.

Numerous incidents of levitation have been recorded in Christianity and Islam. Among the first was Simon Magus in the first century. Other incidents reported among the Roman Catholic saints include the incident of Joseph of Cupertino (1603-1663), the most famous, who is said to have often levitated through the air.

Saint Teresa of Avila was another well known saint who reported levitating. She wrote of one of her experiences: 'It seemed to me, when I tried to make some resistance, as if a great force beneath my feet lifted me up. I know of nothing with which to compare it; but it was much more violent than other spiritual visitations, and I was therefore as one ground to pieces.'

Such feats were said to be duplicated by the Brahmins and

fakirs of India. Similar abilities were reportedly shared by the Ninja of Japan.

Brahmins believe that the 'supreme cause' of all phenomena is the 'agasa' ('akasha'), the vital fluid, 'the moving thought of the universal soul, directing all souls,' the force that the adepts learn to control.

Some physical mediums perform levitations. The most famous is Daniel Dunglass Home, who reportedly did it over a 40-year period. In 1868 he was witnessed levitating out of a third-storey window, and floating back into the building through another window. When levitating Home was not always in a trance, but conscious and later described his feelings during the experiences.

Once he recounted 'an electrical fullness' sensation in his feet. His arms became rigid and were drawn over his head, as though he was grasping an unseen power which was lifting him. He also levitated furniture and other objects.

The Catholic Church excommunicated Home as a sorcerer, although he was never discovered to be a fraud like other mediums who used wires and other contraptions to levitate objects.

Italian medium Amedee Zuccarini was photographed levitating 20 feet up.

Controlled experiments involving levitation are rare. During the 1960s and 1970s researchers reported some success in levitating tables under controlled conditions. The Soviet PK medium Nina Kulagina, mentioned earlier, has been photographed levitating a small object between her hands.

Sceptics have come up with several theories as to apparent levitation including hallucination, hypnosis, or fraud. Eastern believers theorise the existence of a universal force which belongs to another, non-material reality, and manifests itself in the material world.

In everything we have discussed so far involving unseen energies or entities there is a common factor - they are perceived, manipulated or interacted with via the human mind.

Our brains, which look rather like a walnut, are split into two separate halves. The left side contains the 'I' of the personality and is the driver in charge of the practicalities of life while the right lobe is the dreamer and is the seat of ego-less processes like intuition (and interaction with the Cosmogenic Field).

Usually the left brain dominates, rather like a bullying lecturer who keeps his charge, the right brain, strictly under control. It is when the right brain escapes this domination and is allowed its freedom that the miraculous happens.

Savants

As I mentioned earlier, there are many anomalous phenomena that have baffled people for generations. They have happened, been witnessed by many perfectly sane and down-to-earth people, but have defied explanation. But, the existence of Cosmogenic Energy, a swirling ocean of universal knowledge and power, past, present and future, would account for many of them. We've talked about poltergeists. Here's another strange mystery which supports the idea of that computer in the sky - mathematical prodigies.

Five-year-old Zerah Colburn, son of a Vermont farmer in the United States, astonished his father by suddenly performing incredible feats of calculation. The boy was unable to read or write or recognise any number written down on paper but here he was capable of answering questions like, 'What number, multiplied by itself, will produce 998,001?' Within four seconds he gave the correct answer of 999.

Farmer Colburn, who was just about scraping a living in the early 1800s, was quick to see the earning potential and put his son on show. Within two years Zerah was touring the world astounding audiences who'd come from far and wide to witness the impossible.

In England, when he was eight, Zerah was asked the square root of 106,929 and, before the number could be written down in confirmation, Zerah had answered 327. He shot back with the answer 645 when a member of his audience demanded to know what was the cube root of 268,336,125.

There were hundreds of these performances and he still did not know how to multiply or divide in conventional terms on paper! Asked how he did it he said, 'I just don't know, sir.' He said that the answers just jumped into his head. So where did the information come from? Clearly, he did not have access to a computer as they were still to be invented. Was his intuitive right-brain 'tuning in' to answers supplied by the celestial supercomputer?

Zerah was not the only 'human adding machine' to astound the world. In 1976 Willem Klein correctly supplied the 73rd root of a number with 499 digits. In 1789, Dr. Benjamin Rush, often referred to as the father of American Psychiatry, described in detail the lightning calculating skills of Thomas

Fuller 'who could comprehend scarcely anything, either theoretical or practical, more complex than counting.' When Fuller was asked how many seconds a man had lived who was 70 years, 17 days and 12 hours old he gave the correct answer of 2,210,500,800 in 90 seconds even correcting for the 17 leap years included.

These are just three cases where answers came 'out of the sky' via intuition rather than painstaking methodical effort. If nothing else it teaches us that intuition is a powerful tool.

The abilities of mentally-impaired identical twins George and Charlie were just as incredible. They were brought before the American Psychiatric Association in 1964 to demonstrate their extraordinary abilities. Their IQs were low, they could barely read and could just about add up to 30. However, they could match or beat the best computers of their day when asked questions involving calculations with days and dates.

They were able to name all the years in the next 100 in which Easter would fall on 23 March and all the years in the next 20 when 4 July would be a Tuesday. The so-called 'calculating twins' could span over 40,000 years backward or forward in time and tell you, instantly, what days of the week any date was, or would be.

One observer with his own 100 year calendar asked what 22 January 2042 would be and George instantly replied, correctly, 'Wednesday.' Asked by another psychiatrist which years in the past 200 and the next 500 Christmas day fell, or would fall, on a Sunday, Charlie began reeling off a list until he was stopped.

Asked how they did it, George replied, 'It's in my head so

I can do it.'

They also remember the weather for every day of their adult life. Extraordinary.

George and Charlie are probably 'savants.' These people are human beings who are incapable of reading and writing properly, yet somehow have a unique talent in the fields of mathematics, art and music. They do not acquire knowledge by learning but mysteriously 'know' explicit and correct information. Savants have baffled science for centuries. However, their talents fit in well with the theory of a Cosmogenic Field of data which, somehow, their intuitive minds tap into.

The physician, the late Oliver Sacks describes in his book *The Man Who Mistook His Wife For A Hat* twins John and Michael, who were able to define prime numbers up to 20 digits. Yet they could barely make the simplest additions and subtractions. Asked to explain their ability they replied, 'We just see the numbers in our heads.'

A UK savant who gained widespread celebrity is Daniel Tammet who was born in London, in 1979. After a series of epileptic seizures as a child, which seemed to re-wire his brain, he was able literally to 'see' numbers in his head, as swirling shapes, patterns and colours.

In March, 2004, at the Museum of the History of Science in Oxford, he set a new British and European record when he recited the mathematical constant Pi from memory to 22,514 decimal places.

He can memorise 1,000 numbers in minutes then recite

them backwards and calculate from your birth date the day of the week you were born. Asked by a newspaper reporter what 37 to the power of 4 was, Daniel gave the correct answer of 1,874,161 before the figures could be tapped into the calculator.

Explaining how numbers form in his mind he says, 'I see shapes, textures or moving lights like a child's kaleidoscope. Number one is a very bright white light and two is a shifting movement from left to right. Some numbers are really beautiful - 89 is like falling rain.

'If I am asked to multiply 48 by itself four times I see the shapes of the numbers with the answer as a separate shape between them - like a missing piece of a jigsaw.'

Professor Allan Snyder, from the Centre for the Mind at the Australian National University in Canberra, explains why Tammet is of particular, and international, scientific interest. 'Savants can't usually tell us how they do what they do,' he said. 'It just comes to them. Daniel can. He describes what he sees in his head. That's why he's exciting. He could be the Rosetta Stone.'

Of course it is not just figures that are floating about in our oceans of Cosmogenic consciousness. We are awash with all creation. Our minds can reach out and touch thoughts, ideas, emotions, feelings, dreams, hopes, visions, from the past, present and future. From where did Michaelangelo get his inspiration? Shakespeare his imagination? Einstein his theories? Plato his philosophies?

Case studies appear to point to the right brain as the 'receiver' of the information. The skills most often seen in savants were found to be those associated with the right hemisphere of the brain and those most lacking were those associated with the left hemisphere. The right brain compensating for the left brain's disabilities seems to 'cause' the unique talents.

When Mozart was asked where his music came from he replied, 'Tunes just walk into my head, often too many to write down.' Were all these legendary figures reaching into the Infinite Mind with their minds? Tuning into the celestial transmitter for matter just right for them? Is there information out there with our name on it just waiting for us to tune into the right position on the dial?

Neuroscientists, psychiatrists, psychologists and all manner of learned luminaries have wrestled for decades with the question of How? How do these savants do it? I believe the answer is simple: they access via their right, intuitive, brains the vast, invisible, encyclopaedia of knowledge floating about in the Cosmogenic Field in which we are all immersed.

Apart from Dr Rupert Sheldrake and his followers, modern science is still not yet ready to embrace this idea.

Dr Darold A Treffert, Clinical Professor in the Department of Psychiatry at the University of Wisconsin Medical School, Madison, proposes that the extraordinary, unlearned talents of savants could be down to ancestral or genetic memory.

He asks, 'How does the prodigious musical savant have access to the vast rules and syntax of music - something professional musicians spend a lifetime trying to learn - when he or she, otherwise disabled and often with severe visual loss, cannot read a sheet of music and has never had a music lesson?

'How is it possible for the mathematical savant, with no formal training and substantial cognitive dysfunction, to compute 20 digit prime numbers with apparent innate access to the complex rules and syntax of mathematics, yet fail at the simplest of addition or multiplication problems?

'How can a patient such as that described by A Dudley Roberts in 1945 - post-encephalitic, paralysed with no useful language and a measured IQ of eight, who needs to reply to calendar calculating questions by only grunts and gestures, correctly calendar calculate and tell the day of the week over a 30 year time span by staring at the ceiling?'

Dr Treffert says, 'To explain the prodigious savant particularly, with such innate access to the vast syntax and rules of art, mathematics, music and even language, in the absence of any formal training and in the presence of major disability, a third kind of memory capacity – "ancestral" or "genetic" memory - seems to me, must exist along with the cognitive/semantic and procedural/habit memory.'

Perhaps the idea of an ocean of knowledge, transmitted via billions of different frequencies, and accessible to our human brains, is too close to mumbo-jumbo for him.

However, proposing the genetic transmission of sophisticated knowledge is almost as hard to swallow. And although he prefers to root his theory in the familiar territory of genes and DNA, it is not a million miles from Jung's Collective Unconscious, a concept of inherited traits, intuitions and collective wisdom of the past.

Treffert points out that the idea of a genetic memory is not new.

Dr. William Carpenter, in comparing Zerah Colburn's calculating powers to Mozart's mastery of musical composition, defined these 'intuitions' as 'congenital gifts.'

In his book *The Mind's Past*, Michael Gazzaniga states: 'The vast human cerebral cortex is chock full of specialized systems ready, willing and able to be used for specific tasks. Moreover, the brain is built under tight genetic control.'

He speculates that as soon as the brain is built, it starts to express what it knows, what it comes with 'from the factory.' He says that the number of special devices that are in place and active is staggering. 'Everything from perceptual phenomena to intuitive physics to social exchange rules comes with the brain. These things are not learned; they are innately structured. Each device solves a different problem... the multitude of devices we have for doing what we do are factory installed; by the time we know about an action, the devices have already performed it.'

As Dr. Carpenter observed, 'persons with savant syndrome, particularly the prodigious savant, do show congenital aptitude for certain mental activity, which showed itself at so early a period as to exclude the notion that it could have been acquired by the experience of the individual.'

So how did they come by their extraordinary knowledge? Dr Treffert suggests that ancestral or genetic memory is the answer. I say it's the Cosmogenic Information Field in action.

Returning for a moment to the world of quantum reality,

where it appears that man's mind conjures whatever future reality is in place (particles behave like waves when 'desired' to): there is another remarkable experiment that suggests that humans are not the only creature that can affect events.

In his book *Dogs That Know When Their Owners Are Coming Home* Rupert Sheldrake quotes the work of French researcher Rene Peoc'h whose experiments with day old chicks demonstrated their ability to control the workings of a machine.

If chicks are hatched in an incubator they bond with the first thing they see and treat it as if it's their mother. This natural process is known as 'imprinting.' Peoc'h made a small robot on wheels designed to move in random directions. In controlled experiments the robot traced out a totally haphazard pattern. Then Peoc'h exposed the chicks to the machine, which they 'imprinted' as their mother and began following it around.

After a while Peoc'h stopped them doing so by putting them in a cage at one end of the room. As they could not now follow their 'mother' they made their 'mother' move to them! Amazingly, their need of the robot somehow influenced the machine to traverse the length of the room and then trace patterns up and down in front of the chicks' cage. Their strong desire was reaching out through the Cosmogenic Field to influence not other animals but an inanimate machine.

Now, do you regard yourself as being in the hands of fate? Or in control of your own destiny? What is right for us in the eternal scheme of things is our Destiny. Fate is what happens when our hearts and minds have surrendered to lower forces and the fog that this surrounds us with obscures the forces of destiny.

While nothing in the universe happens by accident and everything is 'meant to be', this does not mean that we are all doomed to be automatons, blundering blindly along waiting for death to bring the whole charade to an end. We all have a choice.

We can choose what our minds receive from the Cosmogenic Field. And we can decide what actions will follow. And we can choose what we transmit back. And all our choices are stored in that metaphorical computer database in the sky – the Akashic Record.

And sometimes, perhaps when we are tired of fighting our lone battle against a seemingly implacable foe, Destiny gives us a nudge to remind us we are not alone. There is a Higher Power in command after all and all we have to do is trust, and know it is so.

The most personally dramatic reminders of this truth are presented to us through synchronicities - those meaningful co-incidences involving people, places, events and objects that come into our lives at the exact moment to fulfil a personal need.

The word synchronicity was coined by Carl Jung, who believed the traditional notions of causality were incapable of explaining some of the more improbable, and often insightful, coincidences.

Implicit in his concept of synchronicity was his belief in the ultimate 'oneness' of the universe.

He said this underlying connectedness manifests itself through meaningful coincidences that cannot be explained by cause and effect. Such synchronicities occur, he theorized, when a strong need arises in the psyche of an individual.

The sort of synchronicity that fills us with wonder and makes us feel that, perhaps, there is something in the guardian angel theory, is when we think of someone we haven't spoken to for years and the phone rings and it's them. Or needing a vital piece of information, a book falls open at the exact page. I had exactly this type of experience when I was researching this book.

I was looking through a Reader's Digest tome called How It Is Done, an illustrated compendium explaining the practicalities behind the marvels of everyday life. I was vaguely hoping I might find some story of synchronicity that I could add to my files. There was nothing. But as I idly flipped through the pages while listening to the radio I happened on a section about how film-makers create special effects. There was a picture of Superman, played by actor Christopher Reeve, with an explanation of the techniques used to create the effect of flying.

As a result of a riding accident Reeve was paralysed and had become even more celebrated as a paraplegic with an unquenchable spirit and a determination to confound all the medical specialists and, one day, walk again. As I gazed at his photograph as the invincible Superman his voice appeared out of my radio. He was being featured on the BBC Radio 4 programme Pick of the Week talking about his recent battle against a virus which was attacking his immune system and setting back his determination to beat his paralysis. Sadly, he was to die shortly afterwards of a viral infection.

While the Reader's Digest publication contained nothing on the subject of synchronicity, it was as if some guiding intelligence was saying, 'Why put up with an illustration second hand. Here's an example of synchronicity personal to you.'

And this was also a reminder that the more you are tuned into the possibility of synchronicities in your life, the more they seem to happen. William Temple, when he was Archbishop of Canterbury, was discussing whether prayers that had produced life-changing effects, were merely co-incidences. He told his interlocuter, 'You know, the funny thing is the more I pray, the more co-incidences seem to happen.'

Tuning in to the Cosmic Consciousness seems to work. Try it. Walk in awareness and you'll find that there is a Plan especially for you. In fact it is a constant awareness of a power beyond ourselves that integrates us into that power.

Psychiatrist James McHarg relates how he was having lunch at his brother-in-law's house when the phone rang. As he was nearest to the instrument he picked it up and a voice asked, 'Is that Ward 2?' Despite being told it was not a hospital the caller said he needed to speak to Dr McHarg urgently. The doctor then recognised the voice of a patient's husband. 'How on earth did you know to call me here,' asked a mystified Dr McHarg.

'I wasn't sure of the hospital's number, so I just dialled the first figures that came into my head,' the man replied.

Occasionally synchronicities have no special significance

except to prove that, if there is a supreme intelligence behind them, it has a sense of humour. It's as if the Cosmic Joker is telling us to 'lighten up, it'll all work out OK in the end.' An example of this occurred to Essex police constable Peter Moscardi. When his station's telephone number was changed he gave it to a friend, not realising that he had transposed two of the numbers.

While on night duty he found the door of a factory open and a light on in the manager's office. While investigating for intruders the phone rang. He picked it up and it was his friend - ringing the wrong number he'd been given.

As Jung expressed it, the synchronicity phenomenon betrays a 'peculiar interdependence of objective elements among themselves as well as with the subjective (psychic) states of the observer or observers.' Jung claimed to have found evidence of this interdependence, not only in his psychiatric studies, but in his research of esoteric practices as well.

As examples he cited the I Ching, a Chinese method of divination which he regarded as the clearest expression of the synchronicity principle, and astrology, the art of foretelling the effect of the stars on earthly affairs.

In a letter to his friend and fellow psychiatrist Sigmund Freud dated 12 June 1911 he wrote: 'My evenings are taken up largely with astrology. I make horoscopic calculations in order to find a clue to the core of psychological truth. Some remarkable things have turned up which will certainly appear incredible to you...I dare say that we shall one day discover in astrology a good deal of knowledge that has been *intuitively projected into the heavens.*' (my italics).

In formulating his synchronicity principle, Jung was much taken with the 'new' physics of the twentieth century, including the Quantum Theory, which had begun to explore the possible role of consciousness in the physical world.

Jung believed that matter and consciousness - far from operating independently of each other - are, in fact, interlinked in an essential way, functioning as complementary aspects of a unified reality.

This chimes in with the proposition of a Cosmogenic Energy Field to which we contribute and from which we draw inspiration.

Some scientists today are coming round to the conclusion that the isolation and separation of objects from each other is an illusion and that everything - neutrons, protons, electrons, atoms, cells, molecules, plants, animals, people - are all part of a flowing web of interaction.

This supports scientist James Lovelock's Gaia Theory which proposes that planet Earth is a living organism, the seemingly random processes of which work intelligently together to regulate and maintain life. In tune with this theory is the startling research which proved that after devastating conflicts, like World War 1, more males were born than females. The Earth is a self-balancing organism.

Sheldrake would go further and suggest that the entire universe is such an organism and that everything in it is designed to maintain a celestial balance.

He cites the termite mound as an analogy of the superorganism concept of animal societies, which dominated behavioural biology until about the early 1960s, when there was a shift in favour of the idea that society was merely a series of interactions among genetically-programmed individuals.

However, he and I believe the superorganism concept is closer to the truth. Atoms, molecules, crystals, organelles, cells, tissues, organs, organisms, societies, ecosystems, planetary systems, solar systems and galaxies are all subject to energy fields, operating within one vast energy field, creating a harmony and balance throughout all life.

In fact every molecule in the universe resonates at its own, unique frequency which acts as both a driving force and a means of communication. Individual cells speak to each other in oscillating frequencies.

In a termite mound individuals each have their roles to play to ensure the well-being of the whole. They are born, nurtured, work, eat, rest, and die. During this process, which matches any animal society, they carry out their functions as if directed by the equivalent of an invisible termite foreman who ensures everything runs smoothly.

The Field Theory explains how termites build adjacent columns, connected by arches the two sides of which meet at exactly the right place in the middle. Termites are blind, and the inside of the nest is dark, so they can't do it by vision. Edward O Wilson, the founder of sociobiology, considers it unlikely that they do it by hearing or acoustic methods, because of the constant background of sound caused by the movement of termites within the mound.

Wilson, who represents the 'genetically-programmed individual' school of thought, hypothesises that they do it by smell. And even he agrees that that seems far-fetched.

Sheldrake proposes that the column construction is going on within a social morphic field, which embraces the whole nest and which contains a template of the future arch. And this proposition is supported by a unique experiment carried out in the 1920s by South African biologist Eugene Marais.

In his book *The Soul of The White Ant*, he describes experiments in which he hammered a large steel plate through the centre of a termite mound. The termites repaired the mound on both sides of the steel plate, building columns and arches. Their movements were co-ordinated and, even though they approached the wall from different sides, the arches met either side of the steel plate at exactly the right position as if nothing had blocked their way.

This, says Sheldrake, seemed to demonstrate that there was some kind of co-ordinating influence which was unaffected by outside intervention. Obviously, smell was not the answer, as Wilson suggests, since even termites can't smell subtle odours through a steel plate.

So, if societies ebb and flow in tune with a wider orchestration of human affairs, and every human has a part to play, how do we maintain our individuality? And how do we achieve happiness, contentment, serenity and a sense of fulfilment?

By knowing what our destiny is and going for it, while being constantly aware that there is a power out there ready and waiting to give us a helping hand. We are getting messages all the time--everything is talking to us and we must walk in awareness. And listen.

So our destiny awaits, if we can 'tune in' and avoid being deflected by those lower forces out to throw us off course.

Q: If all these invisible resources are really floating about 'out there' ready to be plucked from the sky, why aren't more people using them to make fortunes predicting the results of horse races or on the stock market?

A: It sounds like you expect the Cosmogenic Field to behave as your own personal genie of the lamp. You need to treat your knowledge of the Cosmogenic Field with respect and 'tune in' firstly to make your own unique contribution of positive energy for the benefit of the Field itself.

Q: But you've been saying that people are using the energies for evil purposes - the spread of terrorism and so on - so why can't I use it for good purposes, like improving my bank balance?

A: Because improving your fortunes is not a good purpose, it's selfish and selfishness is negative.

Q: So what's the point of believing in a Cosmogenic Field if I can't use its powers to improve my life?

A : You can improve your life, but on the Field's terms not yours.

Q: I don't understand

A: When you get in tune with the Infinite you should not ask for money but, rather, desire an inflow of positive energies which will balance the conditions of your life. Good things will then follow.

Q: So, I've got to make the effort, reach out in a spirit of humility and contact with the Cosmogenic Field will happen?

A: Exactly.

Thought worth pondering: It is the job of a doctor to amuse his patients until they get better on their own

5 PLUGGING INTO THE POWER

ALTERED STATES, TRANCE, HYPNOSIS, GANZFELD, RITUAL, DRUGS, BINAURAL BEATS, WALKING IN AWARENESS, ANGELS, CONNECTING MIND TO MIND

Two kinds of reality exist in our world - sensory reality and clairvoyant (spiritual) reality. Both are equally real and shade into one another like the colours of the rainbow. We conduct our normal lives at the sensory end of the spectrum and mystics, poets and the like move easily to the other. Ordinary people can also make the transition by acquiring an 'altered state.'

The real you is the spirit entity that exists within your physical body. This spirit entity is a collective body of energy connected to a greater sea of similar energy - the Life Force. The Life Force is that energy that governs the galaxies and all universes and dimensions. To make any worthwhile progress you need to sink your spiritual energy into that sea and take guidance from it.

Thought is energy and energy is thought. Belief (confidence) + desire + strong visualisation + emotion + repetition = effect. Emphasise the positive. Begin each day with a positive affirmation which draws towards you positive vibrations. Create a higher vision of yourself that you would aspire to, and hold to this vision day by day. Think, act and speak as if you were that higher self. Walk in awareness of this hourly struggle.

Our thoughts should be of positive things - love not hate, giving not receiving, positive not negative.

Beware of negative forces that will resist this change. Fight back. The forces of resistance will create the illusion that you are deluding yourself. It will appear your positive thinking is producing negative results. This is the way negative entities conduct their fight - by undermining your confidence. Once they get a foothold you'll start to slip.

So ignore the apparent paradoxes they're creating and stick to your beliefs. Thinking positive IS working. Give it time. Give it your confidence. You'll win in the end if you stick with it. While you are assailed by doubt, ignore it and sail serenely on.

The Cosmogenic Field of energies comprise the whole spectrum of resonances, from horror, fear, anguish, hate, lust - to love, happiness, confidence, unselfishness, caring etc. Our minds are being bombarded continually. When tempted to lower your standards do the opposite. Don't forget your tools are thoughts, words and deeds which are always creating.

Where the mind goes, life energy follows. As we've seen, human thought creates a field of intention which can influence people, animals and random events.

It has been proved in numerous scientific experiments that human intention can affect bacteria, yeast, plants, ants, chicks, mice and rats, cats and dogs, human cells and even the brain rhythms of other human beings where the most ordered mind prevails. This adds support to Sheldrake's notion of ideas spreading via morphic resonance. The signal from one, powerful mind can impose itself on the less ordered brains of others.

The work of Masaru Emoto, a creative and visionary Japanese researcher, reinforces this idea in a remarkable way. Dr Emoto has been photographically documenting molecular changes in water caused by different 'thought vibrations.'

After exposing distilled water to different positive or negative ideas, words, music, emotions etc he freezes droplets of the water and then examines these under a dark field microscope that photographs the results.

His work clearly demonstrates the diversity of the molecular structure of water and the effect of 'vibrations' in the environment on it. The result is a series of photographs similar to those of a snowflake, each with its individual 'signature.' Dr Emoto came to the startling conclusion that water reflects our consciousness.

He followed up his research with a book, *Messages from Water* containing the results of his worldwide studies. The information and photographs in it are compelling evidence that our thoughts affect everything in, and around us.

113

Dr Emoto proposes that even as little input as a word, music or simply meditating on water vibrates the electrons. The resulting geometric patterns demonstrate the very real effect human beings have on their environment. By extension it shows how our awareness and observation participate in the creation of the universe.

If we believe Dr Emoto that human vibrational energy, thoughts, words, ideas and music, affect the molecular structure of water we have to acknowledge the power we have to affect our fellow human beings. Since the human body comprises over 70 per cent water, these same vibrations are having an effect on our own bodies, and those of other people, in the same way as they interact with water itself. That's why it's so important to think positive.

Dr Emoto and his colleagues took their experiments a stage further deciding to see if even words typed onto paper and taped onto glass bottles overnight had an effect. The same procedure was performed using positive and negative phrases and even the names of dead people. The waters were then frozen and photographed.

The different 'influences' they tried included the words, 'You make me sick,' 'I will kill you', 'Adolph Hitler', 'Thank you,' 'Love and appreciation' and 'Mother Teresa.'

The resulting images showed an identifiable response and distinct characteristics reflecting the vibrations that attach to the words. Those that had responded to 'Hitler' and 'kill' were ugly and distorted while the crystals formed in response to 'Thank you' and 'love' were beautiful and harmonious. Many believe this provides profound evidence that we can positively heal and transform ourselves and our planet by the thoughts we choose to think.

I hope by now you are beginning to be convinced of the notion that thought energy has an awesome power and that each of us has a great responsibility to use that power for the benefit of our fellow travellers, and the world we are passing on to our children.

The idea that in some inexplicable way water retains a 'memory' of frequencies is supported by the controversial work of maverick French scientist Jacques Benveniste, who claimed his experimental findings could profoundly change the worlds of biology and medicine. As a result of his claims he split the scientific community and became one of it most notorious figures.

His journey from respected scientist to pariah began in 1988, when he published a controversial article in the prestigious journal Nature, in which he presented experimental evidence, verified at several other labs, that drugs in highly dilute water solutions can still have biological effects.

Nothing too controversial so far - after all isn't that the basis of homeopathy? But, Benveniste continued with the dilutions until scarcely a molecule of the original substance remained, despite which the water still seemed to have a curative effect. In other words, somehow the water had retained a 'memory' of the drug, or complementary substance, thus supporting the validity of homeopathy, a 200-year-old health practice that is undergoing renewed popularity.

The article caused outrage among traditional scientists who took the view that Dr Benveniste was a headline seeker trying to claim something that was impossible in conventional science. Nature backed off and a debunking team was sent to Benveniste's laboratory to discredit his work. The debunking process was later discredited but the damage had been done and Benveniste lost his lab, his funding, and his position as Director of Research at INSERM, a major French laboratory.

On his website, the redoubtable Benveniste asked: 'Why the fuss, excommunication, resentment, insults, injuries and, last but not least, the crash landing of fraud-seeking commandos? Will the eternal "Understand I do not, therefore it is not" attitude prevail forever in science? Can we not say once and for all "bye-bye" to Galileo-style prosecution and replace it with genuine scientific debate?'

And, in a come-back that surely will be worthy of Hollywood treatment one day, he assembled a private research team around him and continued his work.

And this is where his findings became even more contentious.

Benveniste claimed another seemingly outlandish discovery. In simple terms it was that the unique frequency of any molecule, with which they communicated their 'messages' to other molecules, could be 'captured' electronically.

Benveniste's team turned those frequencies into computer files. The result? The electronic oscillations of, say, a complementary remedy for curing asthma could be emailed across the world and 'broadcast' at water which, as a vehicle for the information, would then transmute into a 'cure.'

Benveniste explained that since there are 10,000 water molecules in the human body for every molecule of protein, the effect was a powerful one. He went on, 'When molecules trigger a biological effect, they are not directly transmitting the signal. The final job is done by peri-molecular water which relays and possibly amplifies, the signal. For example, sound is not directly created by a compact disc. The latter carries data which is audible only after being amplified by an electronic system.'

It is only one step further from Benveniste's findings to believe in Dr Emoto's theory that the frequencies of thoughts, feelings, moods etc could equally be 'broadcast' into water which would then retain an imprint of the original. Or, indeed, broadcast the frequencies into the millions of water molecules in the human body thus creating illness or health.

The apparent ability of water to behave like a miracle liquid is the basis of homeopathy.

This is a centuries old form of medicine that is created by diluting a substance so many times that none of the original could possibly be detected in the remaining solution. Homeopaths claim that with this level of dilution, the resulting medicine does actually work, curing a huge range of illnesses and conditions that, in many cases, cannot be treated with conventional methods.

Medical science says that at such an extreme level of dilution, the resulting 'medicine' will no longer contain even a single molecule of the original substance, therefore rendering it no more than plain water. However, it seems to me that there is a remarkable similarity here to Jacques Benveniste's theories that water can 'capture' messages and Masaru Emoto's claim that water absorbs 'thought vibrations.' It isn't the chemical within the remedy that is retained in the water but the *vibrational frequency* of the remedy.

Here is yet another clue to the powerful effect our thought vibrations can have. So we must ensure those vibrations are the best that they can be and that they resonate with the highest not lowest frequencies.

It is in an altered state of consciousness that we gain access to other planes governed by other vibrations. It is on these levels that psychic phenomena operate. The daily focus of our minds is dominated by the physical barrage of distractions going on around us. But when we shift our focus we become conscious in a different way and open ourselves to resonances in other parts of the frequency spectrum.

Put another way, we have to switch off to sensory information and switch on to the world of the unconscious. Mediums have found that one of the greatest barriers to overcome is the intellect. Successful mediumship depends on subduing the intellect, bypassing the conscious mind. Gaining access to the energy field around us isn't easy. Distractions from our everyday lives build up a shield of resistance which we need to break through.

One method of doing this is to set aside a quiet half hour for meditation and invoke a ritual or personal ceremony that lifts you to a higher consciousness and the 'group soul.' In other words create the right atmosphere to enable you to sink into a deep well of alert receptivity.

The principal requirements for opening our subconscious minds to those other frequencies are: total belief, visualisation, emotion, letting go, being receptive and a conducive atmosphere. And it needs to be emphasised that you are more likely to succeed if you believe that you are connecting to a wider cosmic consciousness.

As we saw with the physicists and the Double Slit Experiment the human mind reaches out and influences whatever is its focus of attention. Believe, believe, believe! Picture, picture, picture! What we picture in our minds, if we do it clearly, confidently and persistently will eventually come to pass.

Thought is so potent that its projected forms can literally shape that outer reality which we believe has been thrust on us by fate, God or circumstance. But, paradoxically, don't strain too hard to achieve results. Use a gentle wishing, backed by a confidence that 'it will all come right.' Intense willing or striving seems to block the effects.

This notion is supported by Sheldrake who says '…if something is done with the confidence that it will produce a desired result, and the participant, once he has done this, psychologically puts a distance between himself and the outcome. He is not trying to make things happen, but just trusts that they will…. Such circumstances may provide optimum opportunity for psychokinetic intervention.'

We all have access to the Cosmogenic Energy Field, but to benefit we must have confidence that we have. Knowing opens the mind to energies right for you. And don't forget, like attracts like so open your mind to good thoughts and good things will happen.

And humour works psychic wonders so laugh at the scoffers. What do they know?

Throw aside fear and worry - instead cultivate determination, persistence, visualisation, faith.

And beware of self-consciousness, which creates a barrier against the Field and prevents it working in your life. It's that left-brain straightjacket wrapping around you again. Shake it off and let the right brain intuit. Don't forget, while the left brain has its part to play, our right brains are our tranceivers with access to the wisdom of the ages and other dimensions. Our lives won't fulfil their potential until these powers are let in.

The very nature of the physical plane conspires to bring us 'back to reality' and away from absorbing the positive energies we're accessing. Submit to the energies and let them purify you. Let them correct the imbalances of mind, body and spirit. Build up the energies that make up you as a human being so that, even after death, they are there intact. Because this earthly plane offers our spirits a unique learning opportunity and what our personalities become here is what becomes our essence as we pass on to the next stage of our lives.

Getting in tune with the Infinite

To say again: accessing the wisdom of the Cosmic Consciousness can only be done by switching off the left brain, with all its preoccupations with the business of everyday life, and switching on the right brain and allowing it to take the stage. All this means is acquiring an altered state of mind. There are a number of ways of achieving this altered state. Below is a selection, any of which might be suitable for you. Each individual has to choose his own way.

Binaural beats

A binaural beat is the brain's response when presented with two slightly different tonal changes in a stereo situation. The binaural beat produced creates an altered state in brainwaves, leading to a hypnotic-type trance or a 'super learning' type environment.

It works like this: If the left ear is presented with a steady tone of 500Hz and the right ear a steady tone of 510Hz, these two tones combine in the brain. The difference, 10Hz, is perceived by the brain, producing the sensation of a third 'beat.'

Research indicates certain changes in consciousness associated with binaural beats. Binaural beats in the delta (1 to 4 Hz) and theta (4 to 8 Hz) ranges have been associated with reports of relaxed, meditative, and creative states and can be used as an aid to falling asleep. Binaural beats in the alpha frequencies (8 to 14 Hz) have produced relaxed but alert brain waves and binaural beats in the beta frequencies (typically 14 to 30 Hz) have been associated with reports of increased concentration, or alertness, and improved memory.

The medical profession is now using what it calls 'brainwave entrainment' in the treatment of depression, low self-esteem, attention deficit disorder, drug and alcohol addiction and autism, to name just a few.

Hypnosis

The father of modern hypnotism is Franz Mesmer, an Austrian physician. Mesmer believed hypnosis to be a mystical force flowing from the hypnotist into the subject (he called it 'animal magnetism'). Although critics quickly dismissed the magical element of his theory, Mesmer's assumption that the power behind hypnosis came from the hypnotist, and was in some way inflicted upon the subject, took hold for some time. Hypnosis was originally known as mesmerism, after Mesmer, and we still talk about someone being 'mesmerised.'

Although people have been pondering and arguing over hypnosis for more than 200 years, science has yet fully to explain how it actually happens. We see what a person does under hypnosis, but it isn't clear why he or she does it. But psychiatrists do understand the general characteristics of hypnosis, and they have some model of how it works.

It is a trance state characterised by extreme suggestibility, relaxation and heightened imagination. It's not really like sleep, because the subject is alert the whole time. It is most often compared to daydreaming, or the feeling of 'losing yourself' in a book or film. You are fully conscious, but you tune out most of the stimuli around you. You focus intently on the subject at hand, to the near exclusion of any other thought. (It seems to me that this is a classic case of switching off the left brain and allowing the right brain to do what it's good at).

In the everyday trance state of a daydream or film, an imaginary world seems almost real, in the sense that it fully engages a person's emotions. Imaginary events can cause real fear, sadness or happiness, and you may even jump if something leaps out of the shadows. Some researchers categorise all such trances as forms of self-hypnosis.

Milton Erickson, the premier hypnotism expert of the 20th Century, contended that people hypnotise themselves on a daily basis. But most psychiatrists focus on the trance state brought on by intentional relaxation and focusing exercises. This deep hypnosis is often compared to the relaxed mental state between wakefulness and sleep (the hypnogogic and hypnopompic stages).

In this special mental state, people feel uninhibited and relaxed. Presumably, this is because they tune out the worries and doubts that normally keep their actions in check.

In this state, you are also highly suggestible. That is, when the hypnotist tells you do something, you'll probably embrace the idea completely. This is why stage hypnotism flourished for a while. Normally reserved, sensible adults are suddenly walking around the stage clucking like chickens or singing at the top of their lungs. Fear of embarrassment seems to fly out the window. But, a hypnotist can't get a subject to do anything he or she doesn't want to do.

Self-hypnosis

This simple technique of self-hypnosis or 'autosuggestion' can be used to improve a person's overall health, boost their confidence or simply as an aid to achieving that 'altered state.'

How to do it

1 Select a location at home where you can sit or lie comfortably in a quiet place and close your eyes

2 Take three deep breaths breathing deeply and slowly

3 Deepen this relaxed state by mentally counting yourself down from 10 to one, imagining at the same time that you are descending in a lift or down a flight of steps, each one deepening your state of relaxation.

4 In this deeply relaxed state, mentally repeat positive statements (orders to your unconscious mind) about what you want to achieve. Be specific - for instance...'Every time I fancy a cream cake, the desire for cream cakes will lessen...'

5 After a few minutes, tell yourself that even when you are 'awake' your unconscious mind will still be carrying out its 'orders' and then bring yourself back to full consciousness by counting yourself back up: 'Three - I'm beginning to come out of my relaxed state,' 'Two -I'm feeling refreshed and alert,' 'One - I'm fully conscious again.' Then open your eyes.

Repeat this technique once or twice a day for a few weeks. Don't expect an immediate transformation. But, be confident that changes are afoot.

Trance state

Trance states are similar to self-hypnosis. It's where you shut out the clamour that keeps your conscious 'left brain' on its toes, allowing the 'right brain,' intuitive part of your mind to tune into 'out there.'

Using meditative instruments are one of the easiest ways to induce deep trance states. These include relaxing music, the sounds of pan pipes or Tibetan Bells and Bowls and the like.

With your eyes open, focus your attention on any small spot or object in front of you and above your line of sight. Keep focusing on the spot and direct all your attention towards it, clearing your mind of all other thoughts and distractions.

Continue breathing deeply and slowly, and begin suggesting to yourself how relaxed you feel, and how tired your eyes are becoming. And this is where the difference comes between self-hypnosis and the trance state. Whereas in self-hypnosis you use your receptive mind to accept 'orders' to achieve some goal, the trance state is where the receptive mind is allowed to receive whatever is 'out there' floating in the Zero Point Field.

Sensory deprivation - the Ganzfeld Effect

Anyone who is trying to learn how to meditate, or is interested in experiencing an altered state, should try The Ganzfeld. This is a state of sensory deprivation produced by covering the eyes with half ping pong balls coloured pink, yellow or blue. Meanwhile, the ears are covered by stereo headphones fed with a continuous hiss, or 'white noise.' Without visual or auditory distraction the subject is said to be in the Ganzfeld State.

Historically, Arctic explorers were the first people to describe the Ganzfeld effect. After they had gazed into a frosty field of snowy white for a while they reported experiencing a form of snowblindness.

Further research in the 1930s discovered that when people gazed into a featureless field of vision (a Ganzfeld), they quickly and consistently entered a profoundly altered state.

When Ganzfelds have been tried by experienced meditators, they have described the effect as instant meditation, whereas most forms of meditation require you to focus your attention on a spot, flower, mantra, etc.

While traditional meditation can take many years of

practice, a Ganzfeld works for most people in a matter of minutes. (Some researchers have claimed also to have tested the effects of Ganzfelds on psychic abilities, and have found a statistically significant increase in test scores). People have reported using Ganzfelds to achieve the following:

Instant meditation

Self hypnosis

Astral journeys

Past Life regression

Psychic abilities

Guided imagery

Creativity

Relaxation

Self healing & improvement

Ritual

This is one of the methods chosen by the shaman in primitive tribes to gain access to the spirit world and its inhabitants. They would also employ other vision-inducing means including drugs, yoga techniques and sensory deprivation. Rituals, just as effective today, involve creating the right setting to shut out worldly distractions and using dancing, drumming and chanting. The rhythm most effective seems to be two beats a second.

Hypnopompic/hypnogogic sleep

This is the 'twilight' period just before either falling fully asleep or just before waking, when consciousness is in a half-way 'between state' of relaxation. A whole range of anomalous experiences has been reported during the hypnagogic (falling asleep) or hypnopompic (awakening) states, like brief, vivid, and often strange imagery. Some find themselves temporarily unable to move or speak during these periods between wakefulness and sleep.

Hypnagogic/hypnopompic imagery has been associated with reports of extrasensory perception (ESP), apparitions and communication with the dead, out-of-the-body experiences, visions of past lives, and experiences involving extraterrestrials.

Drugs

A variety of drugs, herbs and other substances are regularly employed to induce 'trips' and hallucinations. However, some observers claim that whatever is experienced under these influences can never be the truth and that this is only ever achievable by natural methods which do not distort the chemistry of the brain.

Meditation

This is simply tuning into those 'higher vibrations' by quietening our minds, listening to music or exposing our thoughts to other uplifting stimuli.

Latihan

We have already come across the latihan in an earlier chapter. It is the Indonesian word for exercise, the practice of which, say followers of Subud, evokes the reappearance of a primordial power hidden within human beings and all creatures. This power manifests itself in spontaneous bodily movements and utterances, a mood of tranquility and joy, clarity of awareness, and love for the Divine.

It works progressively to cleanse and harmonise the conflicting elements of our being, to heal and to illuminate. Its essential nature is celebration and praise. Adherents say it makes possible an increasingly profound realisation of the Wisdom from which we ultimately spring and in which all things are embraced.

Because this spiritual exercise is entirely spontaneous it follows no pre-existing plan, and so cannot be either studied or taught. It cannot be directed or forced in any way, but is simply received, as a life and movement arising from the very centre of a person's being, in whatever forms are appropriate for the particular nature and condition of the practitioner.

Since the action of the latihan is cathartic as well as illuminating, its manifestations may occasionally be grotesque or unpleasant; more usually they are enjoyable, and at times they are of an extraordinary beauty. But because these manifestations are simply the means by which the believer is gradually transformed, they are all accepted with gratitude and experienced with objectivity and detachment.

Prayer

Perhaps the Christian equivalent of the latihan is prayer, when the mind seeks earnestly to connect with its Maker. This can lead to a profound experience known as Baptism of the Holy Spirit, in which the believer is filled with Divine power.

References to being 'baptised in the Spirit' are numerous in the Bible. Jesus emphasized the importance of the experience.

'And being assembled together with them, He commanded them not to depart from Jerusalem, but to wait for the Promise of the Father which, He said...'you have heard from Me; for John truly baptized with water, but you shall be baptized with the Holy Spirit not many days from now" (Acts 1.4,5).

Jesus explained the purpose of baptism in the Holy Spirit thus:

'But you shall receive power when the Holy Spirit has come upon you; and you shall be witnesses to me in Jerusalem, and all Judea and Samaria, and to the end of the earth' (Acts 1.8).

The Bible makes it clear that baptism of the Holy Spirit is not for the cleansing of sin, but for the purpose of empowerment.

'Then the Day of Pentecost had fully come, they were all with one accord in one place. And suddenly there came a sound from heaven, as of a rushing mighty wind, and it filled the whole house where they were sitting. Then there appeared to them divided tongues, as of fire, and one sat upon each of them. And they were all filled with the Holy Spirit and began to speak with other tongues, as the Spirit gave them utterance' (Acts 2.1-4).

The experience continues to this day, in particular within the Pentecostal Church. Those baptised speak with tongues and have other paranormal gifts like prophecy and healing.

The spirit is invited into a person's life and its appearance is sometimes facilitated with the laying on of hands.

A dramatic manifestation of the baptism experience in 1994 has spread round the world.

Known as the Toronto Blessing it started at the Toronto Airport Vineyard Church on January 20. After a sermon by Randy Clark, a Vineyard pastor from St. Louis, Missouri, people began to laugh hysterically, cry, leap, dance, and even roar as a result of what the church called 'a moving of the Holy Spirit.'

Later, a commentator who studied the phenomenon was more specific about the behaviour of the congregation. He said the event caused 'shaking, jerking, loss of bodily strength, heavy breathing, eyes fluttering, lips trembling, oil on the body, changes in skin colour, weeping, laughing, drunkenness, staggering, travailing, dancing, falling, visions, hearing audibly into the spirit realm, inspired utterances - prophecy, tongues, interpretation - angelic visitations and manifestations, jumping, violent rolling, screaming, wind, heat, electricity, coldness, nausea as discernment of evil, smelling or tasting good or evil presences, tingling, pain in the body as discernment of illnesses, feeling heavy weight or lightness, trances, altered physical state while seeing into the spirit world, inability to speak normally, disruption of the natural realm, electrical circuits blown.'

The Christos Experience

Australian journalist G M Glaskin wrote *Windows of the Mind* in 1974 in which he described a technique for enabling human consciousness to separate from the physical body and travel to distant locations, both in present time and in the past and the future. His system involves a series of exercises during which the subject becomes progressively relaxed and the sense of body image becomes slightly distorted and disoriented. Next, imagery is employed to enable the subject to perceive locations, distant in time and space.

The technique employs three people, the subject and two helpers. One helper sits at the subject's head and, with the soft ball of the fist, firmly massages the subject's forehead in a circular fashion. The other helper firmly massages the subject's feet. This continues for about five to fifteen minutes.

Next, one helper instructs the subject in various visualisation exercises during which the subject imagines first the legs extending and getting longer, then returning to normal, then the arms, and head doing the same. This proceeds until the subject feels that he is able to 'grow' at will about two or three feet.

After the stretching and imaging exercises the subject visualises their own front door, taking care to look closely at all its features, and describes what they see. The helper then takes the subject mentally up above their house, in several stages, to visualise the location from different heights. The subject is then instructed to change the time of day from dark to sunny and back again so that they feel that they have complete control of the situation.

The subject is then instructed to fly up above the clouds, to travel and to come down somewhere else. The helper then asks the subject, 'Look at your feet. What do you have on your feet?' Various questions can be asked, such as 'What are you wearing? Touch your hair, what length is it? Look at your hands…' etc.

From then on the helper questions the subject as they proceed through the scene, which may be from their current or past life. Other people in the room can also ask questions. The subject usually terminates the experience themselves and returns to the present and back to normal.

In one experiment involving a class of students some relived parts of their earlier present lives, whilst others seemed to talk about lives which were definitely not their own, either in character or time-period. 'Peter' related part of his childhood in rural Canada, while 'Gwen' remembered part of a life as a South American Indian woman. Each student recounted a different experience.

Enthusiasts say anyone wanting to try the experiment for themselves can do so easily. You simply arrange with several friends to carry out a Christos session, each taking turns to be the experiencer and helper. You are advised to have a comfortable, warm place to work, free from distractions.

When rubbing the ankles and the forehead use light, circular motions. Remember that you can terminate the session at any time. And it's important to remember that if you do not like where you are you do not need to stay there but can easily and quickly return to your body.

The Christos exercise can be carried out with just two people: the experiencer with an interviewer guiding the exercise, or one individual can even carry out the exercise on his own.

Inner surrender

This is my own way of tuning into the Infinite. The principle at work is similar to that found in Subud, the difference being that there is no need for a 'chain reaction' from one 'opened' person to another. The surrender establishes a 'one to one' with a Higher Source.

Its essence is an inner letting go which offers a new means of receiving, from the Cosmic Consciousness, direct and individual guidance for the right conduct of your life. Sincere submission will trigger an inpouring of a gentle power which, if you will let it, will guide you along the path that is right for your life.

Relax and surrender with patience and sincerity and the process will begin. Your mind must be in 'neutral' to get the most out of the exercise. Contact is made by creating the same kind of quiet appropriate for half an hour or so of meditation. You should begin by standing (not sitting or lying down). Take a few slow, deep breaths and surrender. Surrender your thoughts and desires and invite the Power into your life.

What will follow over the coming hours, days, weeks, months and, often years, will be a gradual but discernible purification - first of your physical being, then your feelings and emotions and, last of all, your understanding.

The process is available to everyone, Christian, Jew, Muslim, Buddhist, or atheist. The only essential is that you must believe there is something 'out there' that is greater than yourself and that in some way you as a believer are able to come into contact with that Power.

The response in your half-hour sessions may be absolutely nothing at first and this will be the test of your determination, patience and sincerity. Some sign will eventually come. However, you may notice your body starting to move spontaneously, following no required pattern as you might find stipulated in yoga, for instance. The movement cannot be directed or forced in any way, but is simply received in whatever form is appropriate for your own unique nature and condition.

The action may be cathartic so its manifestations might occasionally be grotesque or unpleasant. Just go with the flow of the Power. And trust. More usually the movements are enjoyable, and at times of an extraordinary beauty. You should treat the grotesque and the beautiful with the same objectivity and detachment. Trust.

To begin with in your daily life you may find a flare-up of your weaknesses and failings before you will be able to detect a definite improvement.

What is important in this process is your submission to the will, protection and power of the Higher Force, or Cosmic Consciousness, or Supreme Being, or whatever you are comfortable with calling it. The fact is, you are part of an intricate kaleidoscope of energy patterns which have a form and substance and a destiny.

Analysing the power which you are submitting to is merely a hindrance as you are trying to bring intellect to bear where reasoning and thinking is incapable of defining the indefinable. 'Be still and know that I am God.'

On offer to you is the same life-changing power as

described in the Christian Bible where, in the New Testament, Jesus's disciples were filled with the Holy Spirit. Humble, frightened and confused souls became transformed into confident, purposeful people led by an inner guidance and fortified by an inner strength.

In this exercise we receive and experience a working of the Life Force which will change our hearts, our characters and our physical health. Our faults will gradually be erased and what is good and true and real will happen without any help from our intellect, our hearts or our desires.

The essence is the pure and passive 'receiving' of the Life Force. The Cosmic Consciousness does the work; we do nothing. Only surrender. It is from the effects of our sessions of surrender that all else will flow including, ultimately, a fuller understanding of what is necessary for each one of us.

If you can follow this way with sincerity, trust, patience, even in adversity or when life seems stagnating, with a true spirit of submission, you will eventually be transformed as will the lives of those around you.

In this pathway there is no discrimination between the different religions, because what comes to a person is really what is already there within him/her. So if a person is a Christian he will meet with the real Christ in him, and if a Buddhist he will meet the real Buddha in him. The same if he is a Muslim; he will meet the Muhammad in himself.

We humans are being corrupted by worldly influences, our desires, emotions and thoughts every second of the day. We are under siege. Under our own power we might struggle to overcome one defect while 10 new ones grow. Two or three half-hour Communion sessions a week is the way to cast out the imperfections and impurities which dwell in our inner beings. And to point us the way to our destinies.

A shock to the system

Sometimes a physical or mental shock, which jolts us out of our normal routines, is enough to overcome the barrier surrounding our unconscious minds and enables us to connect to the universal energy.

Q: If in the submission exercise, or Subud or any other method of contacting a Higher Force we are supposed to submit and open ourselves, how do we know that we are not being possessed by an evil force? How can we be sure that the power to which we submit is good?

A: We cannot be absolutely sure of anything but I have said throughout this book that it is our choice which thoughts to accept or reject as they come into our heads. If we are inviting into our beings only that which is good and wholesome this will protect us from marauding negative entities. And you, and those around you, will also know that what is manifesting in your life is something good and that it reflects what a true approach to God, Brahma, Jehovah, Allah, Tao or the Life Force should be.

From my own experience and observation I am convinced that the power at work is good but such an assertion is only for me. You will have to make up your own mind.

Q: How do I know which method of attaining an altered state is best for me?

A: It's probably a matter of trial and error. Having said that, your instincts will guide you as to which you feel most comfortable with. Choose the top three and experiment.

Q: Even if I do manage to set aside half an hour a day for meditation any calming of my inner being is soon swamped by stress and tension as the reality of life takes over. How do I maintain a state of serenity?

A: The more you access the eternal and the infinite in your quiet moments the more the positive energies of the Cosmogenic Field will help balance your life.

Q: Quietening down my inner turmoil will obviously benefit me but will it contribute anything worthwhile to the world 'out there'?

A: As your turmoil's replaced by a sense of calm, this tranquility adds to the Cosmogenic Field and is like pouring oil on troubled waters. The more meditation becomes a routine part of your daily life the more potent this effect will be. Someone once asked Mother Teresa. 'How can I bring peace to the world?' Mother Teresa replied, 'By bringing peace to yourself.'

Q: Should I direct my thoughts during my meditations to try to achieve specific goals?

A: It depends on your personal philosophy. In Subud or the submission exercise, for instance, the only need is to submit and go with the flow. However, some people firmly believe that 'thinking positive' is more beneficial. For instance In the film *What the Bleep Do We Know!?* Joe Dispenza describes his practice of consciously creating his day:

'I wake up in the morning, and I consciously create my day the way I want it to happen. Sometimes…it takes me a little bit to settle down, and get to…where I am actually intentionally creating my day…then out of nowhere, little things happen that are so unexplainable, I know they are the process or the result of my creation. We're consciously, from a spiritual standpoint, throwing in the idea that our thoughts affect our reality or affect our life.'

He goes on, 'I have this little pact…I say, "I'm taking this time to create my day and I'm infecting the Quantum Field. Now, if it is a fact, that the observer's watching me the whole time that I am doing this, and there is this spiritual aspect to myself, then show me a sign today that you paid attention to any one of these things that I created.

'Bring them in a way that I won't expect, so I'm surprised at my ability to be able to experience these things and make it so I have no doubt that it's come from you." 'And so, I live my life all day long thinking about being a genius…and as I do that, during parts of the day, I'll have thoughts that are so amazing, that cause a chill in my physical body, that have come from nowhere.'

Thought worth pondering: 'The Great truths of life are made known only to those prepared to accept them.'

6 USING THE POWER

HEALING, MEDIUMSHIP, ASTRAL PROJECTION, SCRYING, LIFE-COACHING, ENTITY RELEASE

Firstly, don't forget that psychic skills often evaporate when confronted with scepticism so it's essential to cultivate unassailable self-confidence. Laugh at the scoffers. Paranormal powers operate most effectively when the conscious ego is relaxed (the left brain gives the orders and the right brain carries them out). So, the harder you try the less successful you will be.

Returning to the spectrum analogy, where different shades of reality merge into one another, it seems that when we focus on the everyday mundanities of life we limit ourselves to a narrow band of that spectrum. But when we feel relaxed and interested in the wider world (like when we go on holiday, for instance) we broaden our bands. And this gives us access to a range of practical options for using the power.

Healing

Spiritual healing, faith healing, the laying on of hands, distance healing are all forms of tapping into the Life Force Energy, sometimes referred to as 'Chi' or 'Prana'. The practitioner channels this force to heal both physical and mental afflictions.

Physician Randolph Byrd carried out a random, double-blind study to discover whether remote prayer had any effect. He divided 400 patients into two groups, one half were prayed for and the other half weren't. He was careful to ensure that there was no statistical difference in their illnesses before treatment. He found that after treatment those who had received distant healing had significantly improved, compared with the control group.

Psychiatrist Elisabeth Targ carried out a similar experiment but this time did not confine herself to using Christian prayer. She assembled an eclectic mix of healers from a Jewish kabbalist and crystal healer to a native American shaman and Chinese Qigong Master. She discovered that it did not matter what kind of healing method was used it was the *intention* to heal that counted.

And this is exactly what healer and author Bill Bengston found when he carried out an experiment in distant healing. He gathered together a varied selection of people willing to adopt a healing intent. He then placed samples of hair, nail clippings and fur from sick animals who were hundreds of kilometres away, in different envelopes some of which, to add to the double-blind effect, were actually empty. None of the healers knew which envelopes had samples and which didn't. The volunteers got themselves into a healing frame of mind sending out positive vibrations while the envelopes were randomly dropped into their hands by a machine. Afterwards, Bengston was amazed to find that the healing thoughts had had a positive effect, even though the healers only contact with the 'patients' was to hold an envelope.

'We found that it did not matter if the healers were particularly sensitive or had the empathy of bricks, the healing INTENT seemed to work just the same.' My analysis of this curious experiment is that perhaps the illness was reaching out for a cure rather than the cure being 'sent' from a healing source. Not such a bizarre idea if you go along with the belief that everything in the universe is connected.

Conventional medics don't generally have any truck with what they regard as mumbo-jumbo. And yet the world of wackiness is encroaching more and more into modern healing in the form of alternative remedies.

A better way of curing people. This has been the goal of medical practitioners down the ages. And it has been the seductive claim of snake oil salesmen through the millenia. There have been notable milestones on this exploration, like the discovery of penicillin and insulin and decoding DNA.

Meanwhile, complementary therapists have played their part too in bringing relief with techniques like acupuncture, homeopathy and reiki.

Healing sickness and disease is in everyone's interest (except, perhaps Big Pharma!). Conventional doctors seek to restore their patients to full health. As do complementary practitioners who use therapies without drugs to bring relief from the A-Z of human and animal afflictions.

In their contrasting ways, both sides of this medical divide are continually innovating new techniques and products to improve their performances. But they have all taken the stance that they bestow the healing – it flows from them and their skills to the patient with his or her medical need. But what if the Universe doesn't actually work like that? What if the 'laws' of the Universe *are* only suggestions? What if there's another way to encourage people back to health?

Here's a wacky idea, supported by the Bill Bengston experiment - supposing it's the health need that reaches out for the cure, rather than the cure seeking the need? Supposing that all along we have been assuming that we identify the need and administer the cure while what actually happens is the need is in the driving seat, knowing the healing required and where to obtain it?

To benefit from this off-the-wall idea is to BELIEVE in it. Preposterous, you say. This would require some sort of spooky intelligence to be working outside the known limits of science. Intelligence that can assess a situation and devise a course of action. While we sufferers carry on looking for a treatment that will solve our health issue the treatment is actually looking for us!

Wacky ways do work. If you are suffering from any of the thousands of disorders that affect humans, wacky ways might well appeal and could produce a seemingly miraculous change for the better. Think of it not so much as a cure but more of a new you, with a spring in your step and a new optimism about the future. But before anything can happen it needs you to step outside your normal way of thinking and embrace this world of wackiness (think of that medicineless hospital in Beijing we talked of earlier). It's the equivalent of what some eminent scientists had to do at the beginning of the 20th Century. Back then, these new thinkers turned the world of science on its head when they invented something they called Quantum Mechanics – the world of tiny things. Now over a century later this revolutionary system points us to a new way of thinking about healing people physically, mentally and emotionally.

By the way, we'll be looking in more depth at this whole quantum thing in Appendix 1 in which I relate the theory to the dowsing experience. If you are a dowser already it might challenge any hypothesis you may have adopted to explain the phenomena of dowsing. If you are not a diviner, seeing dowsing in the context of the quantum world might give you a helpful insight on the subject.

But what has all this got to do with our world of wackiness? Well, there seems to be demonstrable convergencies in both quantum and wacky happenings. For instance when dowsers find water hundreds of meters underground using just a forked stick it could be argued that, in the language of the quantum physicist, they cause a 'collapse of the wave function.'

What this means is that the act of observing (dowsing) somehow prompts the energies that are floating about us as 'waves of probability', to become particles, which then assume a shape and become a reality.

In the land of wackiness we can use this same principle to bring about healing. We can create a new reality. We can choose something different from the millions of probable outcomes. We can bring about beneficial change. We can create a different person – one without the illness, disease or infirmity. We can bring about healing.

In his book *In Resonance With Nature* Hans Andeweg gives a good example of how his mental intention had a physical effect on matter. His talents were often employed by landowners to give an 'energy audit' of their forests. Andeweg would tune his mind into the location of the trees and would be able to diagnose if they were in good health or sick.

One extraordinary manifestation was that if he told a landowner that his trees were in bad shape they took on that bad shape from the moment of his diagnosis. It appeared that the trees were either healthy or sick as a result of his passing a verdict! Andeweg's speciality is energy and he believes everything is either giving or taking energy from us all the time.

'Touch a tree and ask yourself silently if it is giving or taking energy from you and listen to your body. Then do the same with an inanimate object and learn the signs.' He said the skill was especially useful when shopping! The principles he espoused are not dissimilar to those employed by dowsers in searching for water or invisible energies.

That there are energies all around us there can be no doubt. Celebrated healer Matthew Manning was almost expelled from school due to the chaos caused by poltergeist activity like flying objects and moving furniture that surrounded him. When he was 16 this phase ended and was replaced by the curious ability to produce automatic writing in languages unknown to him like Greek and Arabic.

Later still he agreed to allow his brainwave patterns to be measured during psychic activity and his EEG chart showed his Theta rhythms (frustration) in harmony with his Beta (concentration) and Alpha (relaxation). Tested in the US he could kill cancer cells by concentrating, and by the laying on of hands. He could also arouse or quieten hamsters in a nearby room just by thinking about them.

William Braud PhD, professor and research director at the Institute of Transpersonal Psychology in Palo Alto, California, has taken this a stage further. In the context of the quantum world, where time doesn't exist, he is suggesting that curing of present diseases can be achieved by healing thoughts being sent back into the past.

In a paper, Alternative Therapies in Health and Medicine, he says that virtually all medical and psychological treatments and interventions - conventional as well as complementary and alternative - are assumed to act in present time on present, already well-established conditions.

'However', he goes on, 'an alternative healing pathway is proposed in which healing intentions, in the form of direct mental interactions with biological systems, may act in a 'backward,' time-displaced manner to influence probabilities of initial occurrence of earlier 'seed moments' in the development of illness or health.

'Because seed moments are more labile, freely variable, and flexible, as well as unusually sensitive to small influences, time-displaced healing pathways may he especially efficacious.'

The idea that mental intentions in the present could have direct, observable influences on the past may seem like science fiction but it fits in with quantum's non-locality and time displacement. Also with the idea that mind is interconnected with all things in the universe.

Professor Braud says that if these non-local intentions are aligned with aims or goals of health and wholeness, 'perhaps active intentions could be directed in the present or even into the past to promote biological and psychological seed moments favourable to physical and psychological health and well-being.'

Fantastic? Unbelievable? Professor Braud aside, healers are aware that there are both positive and negative energies and they 'tune in' to the positive ones and put up a mental barrier against the negative. The greatest enabler in this spiritual alchemy is their belief. And if you believe the power extends back in time, then perhaps it does.

The healing method that is probably closest to our idea of tapping into the Cosmogenic Field is that of Reiki (pronounced ray-key) a Japanese word representing universal life energy. It is derived from rei, meaning 'free passage' or 'transcendental spirit' and ki, meaning 'vital life force energy' or 'universal life energy.'

Reiki involves the transfer of energy from one person to another to enhance the body's natural ability to heal itself through the balancing of its energies. This touches all levels - body, mind, and spirit.

Those who practise Reiki say it has many effects: it brings about deep relaxation, destroys energy blockages, detoxifies the system, provides new vitality in the form of healing universal life energy, and increases the vibrational frequency of the body. It is similar to spiritual healing except that, in spiritual healing the healer emits an energy field which is transferred to the recipient. Whereas a Reiki practitioner allows the 'patient' to draw to himself what energy is necessary. In the former the healer is active and in the latter it's the recipient who takes the initiative, identifying the need and drawing the energy required. This is very similar to the examples earlier of the illnesses of Bill Bengston's 'patients' drawing healing to themselves from willing givers.

We could extrapolate this to include Dr Emoto's theory that vibrations are imprinted on water. Or Dr Benveniste's claim that frequencies of molecules can be 'captured' by water. And from this it follows that the positive energies flowing in Reiki are 're-tuning' the body's millions of water molecules into a new state of balance and harmony. And don't forget that if water has a memory it 'remembers' the imprint of both good energies and toxins. Goodness knows what effect this has on the population of big cities like, say, London whose tapwater has been re-circulated through humans an average of 25 times.

Vortex Healing

Vortex Healing is a form of energy healing, along the same lines as Reiki. Its origins are said to date back to 753BC, and have been passed down through the Merlin lineage. The present day founder Ric Weinman, a US healer and author, claims the original spirit of Merlin gave the knowledge to him. Whatever its background, Vortex Healing is now supposed to be helping many people improve long-standing conditions.

Vortex Healing derives its name from the theoretical existence of an energy 'vortex' which came about 5600 years ago. It is said to be formed from the energy and consciousness of a man called Mehindra, who after his death joined with seven other beings to bring about a divine 'healing realm.' The powers of healing apparently became manifest when Merlin began to use the gift, and pass it on to other people by the process of direct consciousness transmission.

The client lies down fully clothed and the practitioner places their hands lightly on the head, this may be all that they do, although sometimes they may also place their hands on a specific area of the body where symptoms are felt. A session may last up to an hour. It's worth noting here that all healing systems have their own morphic field and the knowledge and experience of everyone who has ever practised healing is available to anyone reaching out to to the field with sincere intent.

The key is to resonate with the field so completely that you are immersed in it – in the wisdom of the ages which makes itself available to you. That is when the magic – the miraculous – occurs, because you have linked yourself to an enormous database of universal energy.

Vortex Healing is said to be useful for conditions such as chronic fatigue, emotional problems and candida infections. It is also said to work well on physical conditions such as sprains and fractures.

Mediumship

This is the process where a human instrument, known as a Medium or Channel, is used by one or more discarnate, spirit personalities to:

· Present information

· Cause so-called paranormal activities to occur

· Channel energies

·Manifest themselves for objective examination and/or identification

A spirit who uses a medium for the purpose of communication, either verbally or visually, is known as a spirit communicator. A spirit who uses a medium for working with and/or manipulating energies is called a spirit operator. This distinction is very general and a spirit operator can, and often does, communicate.

Mediumship can be distinguished as two basic types: Mental mediumship and physical mediumship.

In a demonstration of mental mediumship, it is the medium who hears, sees, and feels what the spirit communicators are relating. And, it is the medium's function to relate the information, with minimum personal influence and prejudice, to the recipient of the message, also known as the sitter. The medium receives this information under various states of control.

Physical mediumship involves the manipulation and transformation of physical systems and energies. The spirit operators, in this case, are causing something to happen on the earthly plane. What it is that actually happens varies with the style of mediumship involved, but the results can be seen and heard by others.

The gift of mediumship, which can be taught like any other skill, has been around for as long as humanity.

During the Victorian era one of the most prominent mediums

was the earlier-mentioned Scots American, Daniel Dunglass Home, usually referred to as 'DD' Home. Some of the abilities attributed to Home were levitation, bodily elongation, resistance to pain, clairvoyance and, strangely, self-luminescence.

Modern Developments

In the 1970s, during the paranoia of the Cold War, the Russian and American security services raced against each other to gain the psychic advantage. The US military believed that the USSR was developing a system of spying based on the abilities of psychics to remotely 'see' targets. The Americans responded with their 'Stargate Project.'

A prominent individual in this 'black ops' initiative was Major David Morehouse who allegedly learned to project part of his consciousness to any given location on the surface of the planet using a photograph or map co-ordinates as a starting point.

While in the process of projecting his consciousness he described sights, sounds and sensations, including visions of beings he regarded as 'angels.' Morehouse suggested that once in a suitable mental state he, and others like him, could not only travel in space, but also in time to both past and future.

And once again this brings us back to the Quantum Universe, where possibly effect precedes cause and, in a typical example of time paradox, the result could be observed before the action was taken. The apparent impossibility of time travel is becoming theoretically credible as quantum physicists theorise the possibility of manipulating gravity and therefore space/time and creating localised time shifts.

However, as far as Stargate goes, the project was shelved, then abandoned because the results were too hit or miss and could not be properly quantified and guaranteed.

Some of these factors are identical to those described by mediums travelling in the astral plane. Did Morehouse and his colleagues travel this parallel dimension?

Astral projection

The conditions necessary for astral projection are:

· Alert mind

· Relaxed/tired body

· Will

Adepts say the technique is to relax the body suddenly, turn the mind inward, looking at a dark screen inside your skull.

With a strong desire project the mind upwards as if your foot is trapped in a crevice on the seabed and you are struggling to free yourself and swim to the surface.

Strongly visualise your 'target' and strongly desire to be with it.

Persist. Because of the 'like attracts like' universal law your thought forms will attempt to merge with the real target, drawing you to it.

Thus, with the body in a trance state, a strongly-visualised image and a powerful desire, and the will to persist, all the conditions are right, say believers, for astral projection.

Scrying

Scrying is the name given to the ancient technique of gazing into an object such as a crystal ball or darkened mirror for the purposes of divination. Although some people can achieve visions from gazing into flames or even a shallow bowl of water or black ink, the clear quartz crystal ball is the most common method used.

Adherents say anyone can learn to scry. It is all a matter of practice. If you meditate, they suggest, it will be much easier. If you ask a question - and place lots of desire in receiving an answer - it will manifest faster for you.

The amount of time you use for scrying can vary from a few minutes to half an hour.

Though some people go through rituals before they scry, it isn't necessary. If you wish to ask your spirit guides for guidance, say scryers, go ahead. Some people say a little prayer and ask for the correct information to appear.

Scrying can be done with a number of different surfaces which include:

· Water in a dark bowl - or small pool

· Darkened mirrors

· Crystal balls

· Tealeaves and coffee grounds

· Embers in a fire at night

· A dimly lit room or candlelit room - looking into the eyes of another person who sits across from you.

Scryers gaze steadily into their chosen surface until they can pick out shapes or images. These may appear as crude sketches, or occasionally, with the clarity of a photograph.

As the images become clearer, scryers find that they know things about what they are seeing. Background information starts to flow through their minds.

Life Coaching

The person who confidently conducts his or her life in the context of a universe of energies has the right perspective to be a life coach. Life coaching or personal coaching is different from training. Coaching draws out rather than puts in. It develops rather than imposes. It reflects rather than directs.

Coaching is a relatively new and different profession - different from psychology, counselling or therapy in that it doesn't try to offer answers. Instead, it works with people to help them find answers for themselves enabling them to make decisions that will improve their lives.

Coaches are consulted for many different reasons including a desire to climb the career ladder faster, to feel more fulfilled at work, to improve relationships with family and partners, to learn parenting skills that benefit both the child and parent, to gain a spiritual meaning to life, or simply a desire to get life back onto an even keel.

Entity release

What are entities and negative energies?

As we discussed earlier earthbound spirits and dark energy forces are the two most common types of entities. The spirit is the part of us that survives after death of the physical body. Curses, psychic attacks and negative thought forms are negative energies generated by living people.

In order for entities to attach to a human, that person must be vulnerable in some way. An earthbound spirit may attach while the human is unconscious for any reason - a blow to the head, anaesthesia in surgery, the effect of drugs, drunkenness, etc. Severe stress, exhaustion, grief, extreme anger, fear, or guilt can also open a person to attachment.

Some believe that without proper protection, such activities as channelling, mediumship, being present at a seance, or using an Ouija board and automatic writing are open invitations for possession. Childhood abuse, rape or incest can also allow entities to attach.

Entity releasements are done by a range of practitioners including hypnotherapists who are specially trained in this procedure and who have a working knowledge of metaphysics and parapsychology.

Spirit releasement is different from exorcism. Exorcism, usually performed by a minister or a member of the clergy, is an adversarial procedure to cast out demons. In the releasement process, the therapist persuades these attached entities, who are not generally evil in themselves, to go to their 'proper place in the Light.'

In cases of earthbound spirit attachment, the entity is simply made aware of its situation and lovingly guided into the Light, usually into the care of a loved one who comes to help in the transition.

Curses and negative energies are removed by severing connections with the source and transforming the energies from negative to positive.

Some believe that we live in a 'tower of babel' of intelligent energies and our brains have been constructed to filter them out. If they didn't filter, humans would be assailed by a cacophony of competing thoughts which would blow our minds.

Q: Is it possible to be haunted inside your head? Sometimes it feels like different people have taken over my mind?

A: Yes, it's perfectly possible.* While there are different sources for these inner voices mostly they are discarnate intelligences that once lived as human beings but who are now dead but don't know it. To satisfy their previous earthly desires, addictions and obsessions they latch onto the energy field of a living human and to a greater or lesser degree begin to control their thoughts.

Q: This seems so far-fetched. Isn't it more likely that I'm having some sort of mental breakdown and becoming schizophrenic?

A: This could be the case but what is schizophrenia? While the medical profession treat it as a mental disorder, the symptoms are similar to those of a spirit attachment.

Q: I'd like to harness the powers locked up in the Cosmogenic Field to heal or to foretell the future but, surely, it's a gift and not something that can be learned?

A: You don't know what you are capable of until you try. And the first thing you must do is open yourself to the positive energies of the Cosmogenic Field and see where it leads you. Then, like everything else in life, if you find you have a talent for something it will improve with practice. There is an old saying that has survived the test of time: 'What is for you won't go past you.'

Q: But what if I don't have a talent for something? Perhaps some people are just destined to be ordinary.

A: There is no such thing as ordinary. We touch other people's lives every day with the things we do, say and think. You may be fulfilling your destiny in the most unexpected ways. The important thing is to be in tune with the Cosmic Mind and the rest will follow.

Q: I know someone who claims to be a medium, but to me he is very unconvincing. It almost seems as if he is playing on people's needs and makes things up as he goes along.

A: There are many charlatans in the world of the paranormal as there are in all walks of life. But that does not mean that some people don't have genuine gifts of tapping into powers outside of themselves. Believe me, the powers are there but few of us make the time to understand them and build a relationship with them.

Q: If you had one tip to help me tune into the Cosmic Mind what would it be.

A: Believe. Without belief nothing else will follow.

Q: I think I'm a born sceptic and it goes against the grain to believe in what seems like mumbo jumbo. And yet, something inside me wants to believe. Where do I go from here?

A: Take it in easy stages. First, look around you at the wonders of nature and how everything seems to fit together into a pattern. This even applies to the universe itself. Scientists will tell you that the infinitely delicate balance of conditions necessary for life to have been created in this little corner of the cosmos are at odds of millions to one. To me that means a conscious act of creation. From that Creator flows our Cosmogenic Field. That's a logical analysis that a sceptic might like to think about. With others it is easier. Faith is a wonderful gift in itself.

* For those for whom voices in their heads are a daily torment, there is an organisation that can help. It's called the Hearing Voices Network and to find their website just Google their title.

Here's a flavour of what they offer to sufferers:

What Are Voices & Visions?

When we talk about voices and visions, we simply mean someone is hearing, seeing or sensing something that others around them aren't. These experiences can include all five senses, hearing, sight, smell, taste and touch. These experiences can occur in one sense at a time (hearing a voice, for example, or smelling something), but they can also happen in combination.

For some, these experiences can be comforting. For

example, someone who is lonely may really value a voice that becomes a trusted confidant. A person who has recently lost someone they care about may benefit from talking to them at the end of the day, or smelling their perfume/aftershave. Others find these experiences to be a source of inspiration. Authors, for example, sometimes talk about how the characters can come to life and write the story for them. However, for some people these voices and visions can be extremely distressing – criticising, threatening or causing confusion.

How Common Is It?

Statistics vary, but it's generally accepted that between 3 and 10% of the population hear voices that other people don't. If you include one off experiences (like hearing someone call your name when you're out shopping, or feeling your phone vibrate in your pocket) this figure goes up to 75%. So, having at least one experience of hearing or seeing something that others around you don't is incredibly common. Those that have never had this experience are in the minority.

A number of famous and important people (past and present) have experience of hearing or seeing things that other people don't. Without these people, the world would be a very different place. This list of famous people who have talked or written about hearing voices includes: Gandhi, Socrates, Joan of Arc, Freud, Anthony Hopkins, Philip K Dick, John Frusciante, Carlos Santana, Robert Schumann, John Forbes Nash, Zoe Wannamaker and Charles Dickens.

What's It Like?

We're all unique, so it's unsurprising that voices and visions can be equally individual in terms of their identity, content, interpretation and impact. The following gives a brief overview. If you don't recognise your experience here, that doesn't mean you're 'weird' or 'unusual'.

Voices

Some people hear voices talking when no-one is around. These could be like the voices of people they know, or complete strangers. They might hear many voices, or just one. Voices can shout, whisper, be clear or muffled. They can speak in sentences or say single words. These voices can be male, female, genderless, old or young. Sometimes they have names, but not always. Voices can speak constantly (24/7), but they can also utter occasional words or phrases. People can hear other types of sounds too, including knocking, rustling, crying, screaming or music.

Some voices can be positive – providing the support and encouragement someone needs to get through the day. Other voices can be confusing, perhaps echoing thoughts or repeating strange phrases. Some voices can be very frightening, saying things that are critical, threatening or commanding. Voices can claim to have great power and knowledge, which can sometimes leave the voice-hearer feeling scared and powerless. Some voices can leave a person feeling very vulnerable and exposed (e.g. hearing a crowd of people jeering at you, or discussing intimate details of your life).

Visions

Some people see things that others don't. These visions can be very clear and realistic, but they can also include fuzzy shapes, shadows and beams of light. Some people see the voices that they hear, others see insects or spiders. For some, the visions are very complex (like entering into another world). For others, the visions sit alongside their everyday world (an added box, person or animal for example). Sometimes, it can seem as if people or objects are changing shape. Their faces may turn to stone, they may be surrounded by a coloured aura or, for example, their eyes may change colour. As with voices, these visions can be reassuring, funny, frightening or distracting.

Smells

Some people smell things that remind them of their past. This could be something nice, like a loved one's perfume/aftershave or a favourite food.

Sometimes people smell things that remind them of a particularly traumatic experience. For example, someone who survived a house fire may smell smoke when they feel anxious. Someone who was hurt by someone wearing a particular scent may, sometimes, smell this when there is no-one there to account for it. This can be extremely frightening, especially if they don't recognise that this sensory experience comes from the past.

For others, the smell isn't linked to a particular memory or traumatic event. For example, some people smell gas, burning or rotting food. These smells can feel very real and leave them fearing for their safety.

Taste

It can be difficult for someone to know that they're tasting something that others can't – unless they get someone else to try it too. This can make taste experiences particularly difficult to deal with. Some people get a strong bitter taste in their food or drink and, understandably, start to worry that there is something wrong with it. This can lead people to worry that they are being poisoned, or that someone is tampering with their food. Others have taste sensations when they are not eating. This might be when they are hearing a voice, watching a TV programme or thinking about something. These taste sensations can be pleasant (e.g. chocolate or a favourite food), but they can also be unnerving or unpleasant (e.g. something bitter or metallic).

Feeling (touch)

Some people can feel things on their skin when there doesn't seem to be anything there. They might feel something crawling over their skin, tickling them or pushing them. Sometimes people feel something underneath their skin, and this can lead them to feel really worried about what is happening to their body.

Understandably these experiences can be very confusing and frightening. It's not as simple as this, though. For others, these experiences can be reassuring. Someone who feels lonely and hears a reassuring voice may feel comforted if they feel a hand on their shoulder. They might interpret it as a sign that the voice is trying to support them.

Why Do People Hear Voices?

There are lots of different theories and ideas to explain why people hear voices or see visions. These include:

A special gift or sensitivity

Trauma or adverse life experiences

Dissociation

Spiritual experiences

Biochemical (e.g. excess dopamine)

Paranormal experiences

Emotional distress

Physical health problems

Cognitive error (misattribution of 'internal speech')

Individual difference

The truth is that we do not know why people hear voices or see visions. As the experience is so diverse, it's likely that there are a number of different explanations. Whilst this can be frustrating for those who feel confused and would like a simple answer or some certainty, it means that the most important explanation is the one that the voice-hearer themselves finds useful.

It is important not to impose your own belief on someone else's experience – this is fundamental to the Hearing Voices Network approach. Rather than providing a dogmatic view of voice-hearing, we recognise and celebrate a festival of explanations.

Whatever someone believes about their experiences, the most important thing is to find ways of dealing with that belief and finding some sense of power, control and hope within it.

Is Recovery Possible?

At the Hearing Voices Network we use the word recovery to mean 'living the life you choose, not the life others choose for you' (whether those others are family, friends, workers or voices). Many people who hear voices simply don't need to recover – they are already living lives that they love. The voices might enhance their wellbeing, or their experiences may simply not detract from it.

For those who have particularly overwhelming experiences that lead them into the mental health services, recovery can feel like a distant dream. The good news is that people can, and do, find ways to deal with (and recover from) distressing voices. Perhaps more importantly, people can also recover from the situations that can make voices and visions so hard to deal with.

Many people who recover continue to hear voices. Sometimes these voices change during the recovery process (being an ally, rather than an attacker). Other times these voices become quieter, less intrusive or even disappear altogether. Others find that the voices stay the same, but that they are no longer ruled by them. They feel stronger and more able to choose whether to listen to the voices or not.

We have witnessed many amazing journeys of recovery in the Hearing Voices Network. These journeys are, by their very nature, very individual. However, these journeys have led us to believe that no matter how overwhelmed or distressed the person is by their experiences (or whatever labels they have collected throughout their time in the mental health system) – recovery IS possible.

Thought worth pondering: It's the person we are, not something we do, that changes the universe

7 OUT OF THIS WORLD

UFOS, OOBES, NEAR DEATH EXPERIENCES, COSMIC JOKER, PARALLEL WORLDS, ALIEN ABDUCTION, ANIMAL MUTILATION, CROP CIRCLES, ASTRAL PLANE, ANGELS & DEMONS.

No book dealing with parallel dimensions, the Cosmic Consciousness, the astral plane and the like, would be complete without looking at other mysteries that defy explanation. These mysteries add to the panoply of strangenesses, which are part of the context in which our beliefs are set. Like UFOs for instance.

Unidentified Flying Objects are often described as nocturnal lights, cylindrical, saucer, bowl, triangular or cigar-shaped craft which appear to be under intelligent control. There are countless photographs and video footage of bright lights in the night sky, and small, reflective, metallic discs, even detailed craft (which are almost always hoaxes).

Those who have allegedly had close encounters with UFOs describe the craft as being large, up to a 100 feet or more in diameter, with rotating parts, and flashing, multi-coloured lights. On rare occasions, the actual occupants of the craft are seen. However, there is no absolutely conclusive evidence that alien life exists in outer space, or here on Earth.

Earthly evidence comes in the forms of implants which have been found in alleged abductees, crop circles and cattle mutilations. Numerous implants have been removed from abductees but have never been found to be extraterrestrial in origin, or tracking devices of any kind. Some crop circles have been exposed as hoaxes, but others remain a mystery. Cattle mutilations could have many, terrestrial explanations.

Popular culture describes two kinds of alien life forms - the Grays and the Nordics. The Grays are described as 3-5 feet tall, with large heads, thin arms and legs, large shiny, opaque black eyes, and with great intelligence.

The Nordics are commonly reported in Europe and are attractive and usually friendly people who are more like 'space brothers.'

Beast-like aliens have been reported in South America and Africa. These include furry monsters, large blobs, and giant insects.

Perhaps UFOs are a demonstration of the ability to slip in and out of our world from other dimensions. Carl Jung believed them to be manifestations conjured up by the human mind.

Alien Abduction

The basic phenomena associated with so-called alien abductions seem to be consistent worldwide. A Harvard professor, the late Professor John E Mack, attracted vilification and admiration in equal measure when he published research which he claimed proved that people who thought they had been abducted were not mad but were victims of a genuine experience.

Ten years before he was killed in a road accident in London he was an eminent psychiatrist, psychoanalyst and Pulitzer Prize winner whose clinical work had focused on explorations of dreams, nightmares and adolescent suicide.

In one of his talks, on the abduction phenomenon, he said, 'The basics are seeing a beam of light; the intrusion of humanoid beings into the person's life; the experience of being paralyzed and taken through walls into some kind of enclosure and subjected to a variety of procedures with the creation of a 'hybrid' species; the conveying of powerful information about threats to the planet such as nuclear war and vast ecological change; the evidences of an expansion of consciousness that occurs for the people that undergo these experiences, for people that work with them and for those who will attend to what this appears to be about - these all seem to be quite consistent findings.'

He added, 'We are also getting reports from all over the world and learning that the basic phenomenon appears to have a consistent core. I have worked with a South African medicine man, Credo Mutwa, a Zulu leader now 74, who had a classic abduction experience when he was 38. This occurred during his training as a shaman. Mr Mutwa was in the bush when suddenly he found himself in an enclosure surrounded by humanoid beings with large black eyes. He was terrified, and underwent the range of traumatic, educational and transformational experiences (described above). He believes the 'mandindas,' as his people call these beings, are trying to teach us about the threat to the Earth that our mindless destructive actions are causing.'

Parallel worlds

For years parallel universes were a staple of science fiction writers who loved to speculate on the possible other universes which might exist. But now it seems their wild flights of imagination are not so wild after all. Parallel universes really do exist and they are much stranger than even the science fiction writers dared to imagine. Scientists now believe there may really be not just a parallel universe--but there could be an infinite number of parallel universes, and we just happen to live in one of them.

Early in the 20th Century science caught up with the world of the paranormal. Mystics had long claimed there were hidden realms beyond our human senses, full of ghosts and spirits.

The last thing science wanted was to be associated with such superstition, but ever since the 1920s physicists have been trying to make sense of that uncomfortable discovery we discussed earlier: when they tried to pinpoint the exact location of atomic particles like electrons they found it was impossible. They discovered the reality was stranger than fiction. Particles really did have the ability to be in more than one place at one time.

This has led to modern physicists, in particular, Michio Kaku of City University, New York, to postulate an infinite number of universes each with a different law of physics. 'Our Universe could be just one bubble floating in an ocean of other bubbles,' he says.

These other universes contain space, time and strange forms of exotic matter. Some of them may even contain you and me, in a slightly different form.

Astonishingly, scientists believe that these parallel universes exist less than one millimetre away from us. In fact, our gravity is just a weak signal leaking out of another universe into ours.

It all started when superstring theory, hyperspace and dark matter made physicists realise that the three dimensions we thought described the Universe weren't enough. A widely accepted theory is that there are actually 11 dimensions comprising membranous bubbles which ripple as they wobble through the eleventh dimension.

Neil Turok from Cambridge, Burt Ovrut from the University of Pennsylvania and Paul Steinhardt from Princeton believe that when two of these bubbles collided there was a very Big Bang and a new universe was born - ours. This means it might well be that the Big Bang wasn't really the beginning of everything after all. Time and space all existed before it. In fact Big Bangs may be happening all the time.

Crop Circles

These concentric rings and patterns up to 100 feet in diameter have been appearing in farmers' crop fields in England, the

United States, and other locations since the 1950s.

They occur in maturing crops, the stems are partially flattened, and entangled or intertwined. The plants are all bent and face the same direction, clockwise or anti-clockwise. In some formations (the non-hoaxes?) the crops are never damaged, broken, or show signs of forced bending. The plants continue to grow normally throughout the rest of their growing cycle.

Suggested causes include hoaxes, whirlwinds, animals, wind vortices, and crop over-fertilization.

Crop circles always form rapidly at night (within an hour according to some reports).

Animal Mutilations

This global phenomenon has baffled nearly everyone involved.

The first mutilation was reported in Colorado in the September of 1967; the same year that 'Mothman' terrorized and mutilated cattle in West Virginia and a decade before the Chupacabra would be blamed for draining the blood and mutilating goats and other livestock in Puerto Rico.

Most commonly, mutilated animals are cattle, but horses, goats, even deer and household pets have been found dead with one or both eyes, tongue, genitals, anus, ears, udder, patches of skin, or other soft tissues removed. In most cases, the animal is completely drained of blood, with only a few drops or none at all located around the carcass. Organs are sometimes liquefied, and dead flies are found on the body.

There are no tracks around or near the carcass, even when

the ground was soft after rain. Also, the wounds appear to be cauterized, suggesting the use of laser-like instruments.

Theories include Satanic Cults, scavenging animals/predators, UFOs, and government chemical warfare experiments.

The Cosmic Joker

This probably belongs alongside synchronicities, mentioned earlier. However, the absurd happenings that seem to be engineered by some intelligent force often goes further than just co-incidence. Charles Hoy Fort (1874 - 1932) spent a lifetime chronicling the incidents and, to this day, his name is associated with weird and wonderful happenings. They are known as Fortean and modern examples are carried in a periodical named after him called the Fortean Times.

During his researches he uncovered examples of human flesh raining from the skies, bizarre artifacts turning up in unexpected places, stars violating the laws of astronomy, giant clouds blotting out the moon and the sun trembling in the sky.

What does it all mean? Fort drops cryptic, breathless hints such as 'I think we're property' and 'I think that we're fished for. It may be that we're highly esteemed by super-epicures somewhere.'

OOBEs

Out of body experiences are those curious, and usually brief experiences, in which a person's consciousness seems to depart from his or her body, enabling observation of the world from a point of view other than that of the physical body and by means other than those of the physical senses. In some cases people having an OOBE claim that they 'saw' and 'heard' things (objects which were really there, events and conversations which really took place) which could not have been seen or heard from the actual positions of their bodies.

OOBEs are surprisingly common. Different surveys indicate that somewhere between five and ten per cent of people are likely to have had such an experience at least once. OOBEs can occur in almost any circumstance - while resting, sleeping or dreaming. Some surveys show that the majority occur when people are in bed, ill, or resting, with a smaller percentage coming while the person is drugged or under medication.

Motor cyclists have reported finding themselves floating above their machines looking down on their own bodies still driving along. And pilots of high-flying aircraft, perhaps affected by the uniformity of sensory stimulation, (the Ganzfeld effect?) have similarly found themselves apparently outside their aircraft struggling to get in!

More curious still are reciprocal cases of OOBE and apparition: the OOBE subject, aware that he is operating in some kind of duplicate body, travels to a distant location where he sees a person and is aware of being seen by that person. The visitee then confirms that he saw an apparition of the visitor, corroborating the experience.

Common aspects of the experience include being in some kind of human-like body much like the physical one, feeling a sense of energy, feeling vibrations, and hearing strange loud noises. Those who have experienced an OOBE are often profoundly affected often drawing the conclusion that we possess a separable soul, perhaps linked to a second body, which will survive in a state of full consciousness, perhaps even of enhanced consciousness, after death.

Near Death Experience

The conclusions arrived at by experiencers of OOBEs are endorsed even more forcefully by those who have undergone a 'near-death experience' (NDE). It is not uncommon for people who have been on the brink of death and returned following, say, a heart stoppage or serious injuries from an accident, to report a vivid experience of leaving their bodies, and travelling (often in a duplicate body) to the borders of a new and wonderful realm.

Reports suggest that the conscious self's awareness outside the body is not only unimpaired but enhanced. Events which occurred during the period of unconsciousness are described in accurate detail and confirmed by those present. The subject sometimes 'hears' the doctor pronouncing him dead when he feels intensely alive and free from physical pain, and finds himself returning unwillingly to the constrictions of the physical body.

In his book *Life After Life* psychiatrist Raymond A Moody published 150 interviews with people who had been pronounced clinically dead, but had been resuscitated, and lived to tell what happened to them on 'the other side.' The experience of a patient who was in hospital with a severe kidney condition, and had lapsed into coma, is typical:

'During this period when I was unconscious, I felt as though I were lifted right up, just as though I didn't have a physical body at all. A brilliant white light appeared to me. The light was so bright that I could not see through it, but going into its presence was so calming and wonderful. There is just no experience on earth like it.'

In Betty J Eadie's 1994 bestseller, *Embraced by the Light*, she tells of her own near-death experience. After hearing a 'soft buzzing sound,' she felt herself leave her physical body. A deep darkness surrounded her, and she began moving forward through it. A pinpoint of light appeared in the distance. Getting closer, this light - 'far more brilliant than the sun' - had the figure of a man in it.

'Next, I saw that the light immediately around him was golden...

'I felt his light blending into mine, literally, and I felt my light being drawn to his... And as our lights merged, I felt as if I had stepped into his countenance, and I felt an utter explosion of love.'

Another bestseller that year was Dannion Brinkley's *Saved by the Light*. Having been struck by lightning, Brinkley experienced a classic near-death episode. He left his physical body, and looked at himself being slid into the ambulance. The medical technician pronounced him 'gone,' and he saw the eye of a tunnel approaching. It eventually engulfed him completely, and he heard the 'beautiful sound of seven chimes ringing in rhythmic succession.

'Then, I looked ahead into the darkness. There was a light up there, and I began to move toward it as quickly as possible.... Ahead the light became brighter and brighter until it overtook the darkness and left me standing in a paradise of brilliant light. This was the brightest light I had ever seen.... It was as though I were seeing a mother, lover and best friend. As the Being of Light came closer, these feelings of love intensified until they became almost too pleasurable to withstand.'

Brinkley goes on to describe how he gained some remarkable psychic skills after his 'return,' including the ability to foretell certain future events.

The similarities between all of these reports are quite compelling and suggest such experiences are a core component of human spirituality. They can be found extensively in every major religious tradition in the world.

The Astral Plane

This is the parallel dimension that exists beyond the physical world which can be accessed by the human spirit. Or at least this is how it has been seen by shamans, psychics and mediums for centuries. It is accessed through altered states achieved through a variety of methods - meditation, trance, auto-hypnosis, mind-altering substances etc.

Once there the spirit, which retains the ability to see, hear and rationalise the experience, wanders amid a nether world of body-less beings which seem to range through the spectrum of discarnate entities from satanic demon to angels, with earthbound human spirits and mischievous and malevolent beings in between.

But today, in addition to the psychic community, there are more down to earth proponents of this inter-dimentional realm of intelligent energy forms - quantum physicists. As we have already seen, evidence is emerging that consciousness is not purely a function of the human mind existing only as a set of chemical and electrical processes, but rather it is a detectable entity in its own right.

Scientists are becoming convinced that we are collections of swirling molecules bound together by an electrical charge and that we interact with other energy fields.

Once the quasi-religious trappings and ritual is stripped away, then the astral plane emerges as an extra dimension at the sub-atomic level. It also becomes credible that what we assume is the consummate evil embodied by some beings in other dimensions is no more than how they function naturally without any artificial constraints of compassion, conscience or responsibility imposed upon them.

However, as advances in the field of quantum science reduces the world and universe we live in to its ultimate and indivisible component particles, would this be the ultimate physicist's goal, the 'Theory of Everything'?

Angels

The word angel is thought to be derived from the Greek word 'Angelos' meaning 'messenger.' In Christian, Muslim, Jewish and other theologies an angel can be one who acts as a messenger, attendant or agent of God.

Throughout the Christian Bible it is generally seen that the will of God is usually imparted or carried out by angels.

Angels are spirits without bodies, who possess superior intelligence, gigantic strength, and surpassing holiness.

Some believe that angels are countless in number, and

flock around the Universe in their millions and are dedicated to serving the needs of all free will entities so that they may experience the same level of unconditional love as they do.

A fallen angel is often classed as a devil, like Satan himself, whereas a guardian angel is classed as a human guide or protector. Angels are commonly represented by a figure with wings and wearing a long white robe. They are also sometimes depicted wearing halos, which emanate from their heads in a glorious wreath of light, serving as a symbol of divine wisdom.

Angels can take on a variety of different forms. In Ezekiel 1.16-21, Isaiah 6.1-3, and throughout the book of Revelation, they are described as taking on not only the appearance of men but many fantastical forms. A notable example was the angel disguised as a burning bush!

Some believe that everyone has at least one Guardian Angel, and sometimes two or three. A Guardian Angel is a being that is dedicated to serve and to help us throughout our lifetime.

Some even go as far as to suggest you can ask an angel to take care of your computer or to assist in resolving an argument with a friend or relative. There is no limit, some believe, to what you may ask an angel to do for you. Believe in angels and there will angels be.

In her book *Hiring the Heavens* Jean Slatter proposes that there are millions of angelic beings kicking their heels in the heavenly realm just waiting to help us out if only we would ask. She suggests readers recognize themselves as part of the divine plan of creation and recommends simply believing that the 'angels for hire' can help us solve problems, both small ('jewel sleuth' to find missing pearls or 'spiritual connoisseur' to find a great restaurant) and large ('romance committee' or 'spiritual employment counsellor).

The book is based on the serious concept that everyone is part of 'God' and that, like parents, God expects everyone at some point to grow up spiritually and take charge, and that the heavens will support the process if called upon.

Demons

The word 'demon' comes from the Greek word 'daimon' which simply means 'intelligent.' According to Christian scriptures Satan has a personal army of demons to assist him in attacking humans and accomplishing evil tasks. They roam the world looking for people to destroy.

The Gospels and the book of Acts describe many exorcisms where Jesus and his disciples release people from demonic possession. The Bible implies that demons are the same fallen angels that once joined Satan in a heavenly revolt.

Christians hold varying beliefs about demons, demon possession and exorcism:

Some hold that demons are spirit beings who do not have a body of flesh and blood. Since they are fallen angels, like angels they are immaterial and not usually subject to human visibility or our other senses. They are dwellers in an unseen world. To manifest themselves among men, they must possess or control a physical body of a person or an animal.

In the Dark Ages and Middle Ages, demons were thought

able to travel on the Earth invisibly, but to assume physical bodies at will. The same was understood concerning angels.

The modern Christian view of demons is that they are usually invisible but are capable of revealing their forms when it suits them. It is not so widely accepted that demons can make their forms material.

The modern demon is thought to punish those who give in to its temptations by possessing the victim's body and using it against the victim and the loved ones of the victim. Frequently, it is claimed, the possessing demon causes the victim to commit a horrible crime.

Thought worth pondering: focused intention crosses all boundaries of time and space

8 THE ULTIMATE SCEPTIC

'Imagine this ... Imagine a world in which if you love someone enough, or need them enough, your minds will communicate across the world wherever you are, regardless of space and time. Imagine a world in which, if only you can think a thought clearly and powerfully enough it can take on a life of its own, moving objects and influencing the outcome of events far away. Imagine a world in which each of us has a special inner core - a 'real self' - that makes us who we are, that can think and move independently of our coarse physical body, and which ultimately survives death, giving meaning to our otherwise short and pointless lives. This is (roughly speaking) how most people think the world is. It is how I used to think - and even hope - that the world is. I devoted 25 years of my life to trying to find out whether it is. Now I have given up.'

Thus writes freelance writer, lecturer and broadcaster Dr Sue Blackmore, who could be termed the ultimate sceptic because she began life as a firm 'believer' after an Out Of Body Experience. She then set out as an academic to prove the reality of the paranormal. She put the psychic realm under a rigorous scientific microscope after first gaining a degree in psychology and physiology from Oxford University in 1973. She continued her researches, adding to her credentials with a PhD in parapsychology from the University of Surrey in 1980.

Her interests have included memes, evolutionary theory, consciousness and meditation. She practices Zen and campaigns for drug legalisation.

Her career examining all kinds of anomalous happenings resulted in over 60 academic articles, about 40 book contributions and many book reviews. Her own books include *Beyond the Body* (1982), *Dying to Live* (on near-death experiences, 1993), *In Search of the Light* (autobiography, 1996), and *Test Your Psychic Powers* (with Adam Hart-Davis, 1997).

The Meme Machine (1999) has been translated into 13 other languages.

Her textbook Consciousness: An Introduction was published in June 2003 (Hodder UK, OUP New York), and A Very Short Introduction to Consciousness and Conversations on Consciousness (2005 OUP).

So, if anyone is qualified to pooh-pooh the paranormal it's Dr Blackmore. However, I wonder why she should despair having failed to prove the unprovable. Paranormal phenomena is a Will o' the Wisp. By its very nature it's ungraspable. And there is another fundamental factor - the Experimenter Effect. She admits she is what she terms 'a psi-inhibitory experimenter.'

Just by conducting rigorous, scientific experiments to prove there is definitely something to psychic hocus pocus, she has been doomed to failure. Because, as we saw in the Double Slit experiments, the hocus pocus has a mind of its own which seems determined to thwart any attempt to place it in a neat, scientific pigeonhole.

Of the Experimenter Effect Rupert Sheldrake says, 'It is well known among parapsychologists that some experimenters consistently obtain positive results in their research, while others do not. This effect was systematically investigated in the 1950s by two British researchers. One, C W Fisk, a retired inventor, consistently obtained significant results in his experiments. The other, D J West, later to become Professor of Criminology at Cambridge University, was usually unsuccessful in detecting psychic phenomena.

'In these experiments, each investigator prepared half of the test items, and scored them at the end. The subjects did not know that two experimenters were involved, nor did they meet them; they received the test items through the post and also returned them by mail. The results from Fisk's half of the experiment showed highly significant effects for clairvoyance and psychokinesis. West's data, on the other hand, showed no deviation from chance. They concluded that West was 'a jinx.'

Sheldrake concludes, 'The implications of such experimenter effects are staggering. If parapsychologists can bring about psi-mediated experimenter effects, whether intentionally or not, through their influence over their subjects, even at a distance (as in the Fisk-West experiments), then the conventional separation between experimenters and the subjects of their investigation breaks down.'

Leaving aside Dr Blackmore's Dark Night of the Soul it's well worth pondering on her analyses which are spot on.

Of telepathy, PK and survival after death she says, 'If any one of these three possibilities turned out to be true then the world is a fundamentally different place from the one we think we know, and much of our science would have to be overthrown. Any scientist who discovered the truth of any of these propositions or, even better, was able to provide a theory to explain them, would surely go down in the history of science as a hero; as the man or woman who changed the face of science for ever.'

But, I say why do we need to prove something in a laboratory to know that it is true?

Dr Blackmore goes on, 'As Richard Dawkins puts it "the discoverer of the new energy field that links mind to mind in telepathy, or of the new fundamental force that moves objects without trickery around a tabletop, deserves a Nobel Prize, and would probably get one."'

She adds, 'I am a scientist. I think the way to the truth is by investigation. I suspect that telepathy, clairvoyance, psychokinesis and life after death do not exist because I have been looking in vain for them for 25 years. I have been wrong lots of times before and am not afraid of it. Indeed I might add that finding out that you are wrong, and throwing out your previous theories, can be the best way to new knowledge and a deeper understanding.

'I long ago threw out my own previous beliefs in a soul, telepathy and an astral world, but even then I kept on searching for evidence that my new scepticism was misplaced, and for new theories that might explain the paranormal if it existed. I kept going with experiments and investigating claims of psychic powers. Finally I have given up that too.

'I have simply had enough of fighting the same old battles, of endlessly being accused of being scared of the truth, or even of trying to suppress the truth; of being told that if I don't come and investigate x (my near-death experience, my psychic twin, Edgar Cayce, the miracle of Lourdes, D D Hume, or the haunted pub round the corner) that proves I have a closed mind. It doesn't. It only proves that after years of searching for paranormal phenomena and not finding them, I am no longer prepared to spend my precious time and limited energy in documenting yet another NDE, setting up more carefully designed experiments to test telepathy in twins, going over all the reams of published argument about Cayce, Lourdes or Hume, or sitting up all night waiting for the ghost that (because I am a psi-inhibitory experimenter) will never come.'

Dr Blackmore goes on, 'The more serious reason why I have given up is that I no longer believe in the world I outlined at the start. Indeed, I no longer believe that the search for paranormal phenomena will provide insight into the 'big questions' of life - though when I started out on my career in parapsychology I was sure it would. I really believed that studying the paranormal would help me with such mysteries as 'What kind of world is this? What am I? and How should I live my life?

'As the founders of psychical research, perceived questions about ESP, PK, and survival of death strike right to the heart of these big questions. If ESP and PK exist, our minds have the power to reach beyond the body with its ordinary senses and physical limitations. Much of psychology and neuroscience must be wrong because they are entirely founded on the assumption that physical transfer of energy and information is required to produce behaviour, understanding and awareness. If there is personal survival of death then we humans must have some kind of soul or inner self that can survive independently of the body. Some form of dualism must be true, however inconceivable that seems to our present day science and philosophy. The implications are immense.'

Dr Blackmore argues that so too are the implications for how we should live our lives. If telepathy or PK are real, she says, then we might be able to help others with their use. 'Perhaps we should cultivate them, or learn to protect ourselves against their misuse. If survival is real then we must live our lives in the knowledge that there is some realm beyond - where our earthly deeds may have consequences, and which gives some new meaning to our lives here on earth.

'But,' suggest Dr Blackmore, descending into bleak introspection, 'what if they don't exist? Then each of us is a biological creature, designed by natural selection for the survival of our genes and memes; here for no reason at all other than the dictates of chance and necessity, and unable to contact or influence anyone else except through the normal senses and physical processes. Our consciousness, and the perceived world around us, emerge from the complex interactions between brains and their environment, and when those brains decay then our awareness stops.

'Living in a world like this is truly scary. There is nothing to hang onto. It seems to me now that free will is an illusion, and even our precious selves are not solid, persisting entities but ephemeral constructions that change all the time. There is no continuous self who lives our lives, let alone one that could survive our deaths. There is no point in behaving well so as to have our reward in the afterlife, for there is no afterlife. There is only this world now, and our actions must reflect that knowledge. I say this is genuinely scary, though I think it gets easier with practice. And to those who accuse me of being scared of the paranormal, I can only say "try this instead." But asking which you find most scary really is not the point. Fear is never a good reason for choosing one's view of the world.'

She says, 'How then can we answer the big questions? I would say in two ways. One is by personal experience and disciplined observation; trying to see clearly the truth about oneself and the world. That is why I meditate and practice mindfulness. So throwing out the paranormal does not mean abandoning spirituality or spiritual practice. The other is by doing science, and for me the interesting questions now concern evolutionary processes, memes, and the origins of consciousness.'

Finally Dr Blackmore admits there lingers in her deepest self a sliver of doubt about her conclusions.

'What then of parapsychology? The world still might be as I imagined it at the start and because the implications would be so profound I am glad that others are carrying on. The recent resurgence of funding for parapsychology means there are several new labs and many new researchers at work. If psi does exist then one day one of them will find a way to demonstrate it and a theory to explain it. If that happens I shall be back like a shot, but until then, happily, I have given up.'

So applying her own scrupulous standards to the results of her researches, Sue Blackmore has judged herself as having failed. Evidence, evidence, evidence, she insists. But, who can prove that God exists? No-one. But millions know in their hearts there is a Supreme Being and His works throughout the universe are the proof. From the unfurling of a new leaf on a tree in the Spring to the creation of a new galaxy somewhere in the firmament, the evidence is there of an overarching

Intelligence forever creating and building.

The energy is there on tap for all who believe.

9 A QUICK SUMMARY TO TAKE AWAY

Everything in the universe is comprised of Consciousness

Even inanimate objects have a form of consciousness

We are all connected (as demonstrated by quantum entanglement)

Time as a linear process is an illusion. Time is now - past, present and future is NOW. Imagine being in a helicopter and time is a stream winding all the way from the left hand side of your vision to disappear off to the right. Jesus is being born over to the left and a bit nearer is the Battle of Hastings and a bit nearer still is the World Wars of the 20th Century. Immediately below is Today and winding off to the right is the future. But you can see it all at a glance in the NOW.

The entire universe is made up of trillions of jiggling frequencies that fill all matters and the 'empty' space in between...the particles that make up atoms that make up matter are jumping in an out of existence and, according to quantum theory, can be in two places at the same time.

The mind is a powerful instrument whose waves, allied to strong emotion, causes disturbances in this jiggling fabric and can reach back into the 'past' and forward into the 'future' because time is actually NOW.

Because we are connected with everything, influences can work both ways and our minds can be penetrated by ideas floating about in the cosmos. This is how geniuses get their inspiration.

Many of the weirdnesses caused by the quantum theory would be solved by the 'parallel universes' theory whereby every conscious decision 'creates' our reality and sets up 'shadow' realities in other universes where millions of other versions of ourselves pursue different realities. Thus we all have eternal life as, while this dimension's body may die, our other bodies continue in other universes.

Also, if we see our daily lives as being stuck in a groove akin to those on an old-fashioned vinyl record. Occasionally we may 'jump' out of the groove and find ourselves in the groove next door where everything appears normal except for strange, small differences.

All the above may seem paranormal mumbo-jumbo but I am convinced that the very real, earthly phenomenon of electro-magnetism has some link with alternative dimensions. If the universe comprises jiggling oscillations of an electrical nature, electromagnetic instruments could play their part in helping us to control the seemingly random nature of life.

If you have found this book helpful please consider writing a review on the Amazon site because this will encourage others to enjoy it too.

And when you turn the final page, after the appendices, Kindle will give you the opportunity to rate this book and share your thoughts on Facebook and Twitter. If you believe the book is worth sharing, please would you take a few seconds to let your friends know about it? If it turns out to make a difference in their lives, they'll be forever grateful to you, as will I.

The appendix below adds a bit more detail to the dowsing and quantum themes covered but is not essential to read.

APPENDIX – THE QUANTUM CONNECTION (for dowsers and would-be dowsers)

There seems to be a connection between the principles of dowsing and the world of quantum physics. In fact the more I look into both, the more things in common I find. Early in the 20th Century physicists like Max Planck, Niels Bohr, Werner Heisenberg and Erwin Schrödinger shocked their scientific colleagues with new theories that flew in the face of classical physics. The world they described turned the orthodox, Newtonian model of large things, from suns to billiard balls (behaving machine-like and predictably), on its head.

The new field of quantum mechanics, dealing with very small things like sub-atomic particles, was an Alice in Wonderland realm in which the bullet arrives before the trigger is pulled, an object is in two places at the same time and two particles can communicate across millions of miles at a speed 10,000 times faster than the speed of light. No wonder these new kids on the scientific block were seen as heretics. One of the greatest physicists of all time, Nobel Laureate Richard Feynman, said, 'Anyone who thinks they understand the quantum world obviously doesn't.'

Fellow physicist Niels Bohr, who pioneered the study of sub-atomic particles, agreed. 'If someone says that he can think about quantum physics without becoming dizzy, that shows only that he has not understood anything whatever about it.' Bohr's contemporary J.B.S. Haldane stated, 'the Universe is not only queerer than we suppose, but queerer than we can suppose.' Reflecting on quantum mechanics some 65 years ago, the British physicist Sir Arthur Eddington complained that the theory made as much sense as Lewis Carroll's poem 'Jabberwocky' in which 'slithy toves did gyre and gimble in the wabe.'

But the pioneers of the new thinking stuck to their guns and now, over a century later, their discoveries are in common use in laser technology, the transistor, the electron microscope, magnetic resonance imaging, spectroscopy, fibre optics - to name but a few 21st Century applications. But what has all this got to do with the world of Dowsing? There seems to be demonstrable convergencies in both quantum and dowsing phenomena. When dowsers access information beyond their five senses it could be argued that, in the language of the quantum physicist, they cause a 'collapse of the wave function.' What this means is that the act of observing (dowsing) somehow prompts the energies that are floating about us as 'waves of probability', to become particles, which then assume a shape and become a reality.

And this mystical 'connection' between dowser and target is very like the phenomenon of quantum entanglement. Based on the Quantum Theory concept I contend that the observer (the subtle energy dowser) actually creates the reality s/he dowses. Their intent changes the energies around us and conjures form. If true this would mean that dowsing pioneers Hamish Miller and Paul Broadhurst did not detect their legendary Michael and Mary lines at all (see their book *The Sun and the Serpent*) – but by searching with intent they conjured them into being! Perhaps the potential of the lines were there just waiting for Hamish to give them life. And the energies along the lines have been growing stronger as others have followed after.

But that can't be true can it? After all don't diviners 'discover' lines of energy? Or someone's allergy? Through their rods or the pendulum don't they access our intuition, or that 'cosmic library', for the information that lies, waiting to be found, beyond our five senses? Quantum physics tells us...no we don't. Instead, when dowsers say to a client, 'I have found several lines of detrimental energy in your home and some negative energy spirals. I have now removed them and your living space is clean,' they are not being strictly accurate. According to Quantum Theory dowsers don't actually 'find' the 'black lines' associated with geopathic stress, they bring them into being by collapsing the wave function and thus coalescing just one of a thousand probabilities. Reality is just behaving in accordance with the expectations of the observer.

Whoa! That's nonsense, you say. A client may have had problems in their home, or office, for months or years before calling in a dowser as a last resort. So how could the dowser apparently be creating the black lines they didn't even know existed until they were called in? Counter-intuitive though this notion is that's what happens, says Quantum Theory. The dowser 'conjures' those negative energies into being with his own consciousness. The fact that they were causing problems before they appeared to even exist is just one aspect of the weird world of quantum physics, where effect can happen before cause. Those pesky black lines have been floating about their location as waves of probability and only collapsed into reality in response to the dowsers' conscious 'observation' of them.

This would explain why two dowsers find different lines of detrimental energy in the same location. It's their human consciousness that is giving form to their own expectations.

Yet, these lines-that-are-yet-to-be, have been the cause of the mood swings, headaches, arthritis etc in the client.

This topsy-turvy phenomenon is simply one element in the zoo of quantum paradoxes at work. This one's known as retrocausality and posits that cause reaches back through time and creates effect.

To even the most easy-going and open-minded of dowsers, this may seem a hypothesis too far. But if, for the sake of the argument, it is possible, it doesn't negate anything dowsing has achieved or will achieve in the future. In fact, some in the science community would contend that dowsers are among the most effective at carrying out humanity's destiny of being co-creators with God, or however you refer to the Divine - Nature, the Cosmic Consciousness, the Universal Mind or the Higher Self etc.

Dowsers are, so to speak, co-architects of the Universal Master Plan (as are the rest of us if we believe). So what does this mean when diviners dowse the energies at sacred sites? Is the energy there, waiting for them to discover it? Or is it their own consciousness that transmutes the inert wave into 'something' which they call an energy line? By their intention to find energies are they projecting a part of their inner being on the world around them? Are they working in partnership with the rules of the quantum universe? And what about those wave functions that might have been collapsed by previous dowsers? Do new arrivals on the scene just add to the melange of energies floating about the place? Whatever dowsers are doing, many leading physicists would contend that they are creating a desired outcome by causing the waves of infinite probability that exist throughout the cosmos to collapse into the shape and form already in their minds. But where did that shape and form in their minds come from in the first place? Did they already exist in the mind of a Creator, who ordained that his plan would only unfold if human consciousness provided the catalyst?

Cheerleader of this hypothesis was the towering figure of American theoretical physicist John Archibald Wheeler, colleague of Albert Einstein and Niels Bohr and mentor to many of today's leading physicists. Famous for coining the terms black hole, quantum foam and wormhole, he believed creation is triggered by our consciousness. As in the quantum world all time is now, past events and present thoughts interact. To illustrate his point he once told a friend, 'The Big Bang happened because I thought of it and I thought of it because the Big Bang happened.'

Wheeler, who died in 2008 aged 96, was not a nutty professor; he was greatly respected in the world of science, a large section of which now shares his belief that human consciousness is a key participant in the unfolding reality of the cosmos. In a radio interview on 'The Anthropic Universe' Wheeler said, 'We are participators in bringing into being not only the near and here, but the far away and long ago. We are in this sense, participators in bringing about something of the universe in the distant past and if we have one explanation for what's happening in the distant past why should we need more?'

The principle of the 'observer creates reality' is dramatically demonstrated in quantum physics's celebrated 'Double-Slit Experiment.' According to the aforementioned physics colossus, Richard Feynman, it captures the central mystery of Quantum Theory. The Double Slit Experiment was first carried out by Thomas Young back in 1803, but since then variations on the same theme have propelled us further and further into a real life Alice in Wonderland realm. It's almost as if we humans live in two parallel universes with different rules that overlap at the edges.

The best brains in the business have sought to explain the seemingly impossible results of this (in)famous experiment, but so far no-one has succeeded. But, its legacy is a mind-altering view of our world. Dowsers would probably find it easier to accept than many physicists, whose only way of coping with its spooky phenomena is to shut it out of their minds. Dowsers are well used to the concept 'something happens but I don't know why...all I do know is that it happens.' The Double-Slit Experiment is all about energies – the sort dowsers love.

Few scientists these days disagree that everything around us is made of atoms. And atoms are made of energy. This energy comprises electrons, protons and neutrons called particles, which are popping in and out of existence constantly. Scientist don't know why or where they go. They just know they are elusive but are definitely there. If they weren't there we wouldn't be here. A particle is what we perceive as matter of some sort - something with mass like tables and chairs, buildings, mountains, elephants. You and I are made of particles. But a particle is a quantum Jekyl and Hyde and has another self lurking in its being called a wave, which is an undulating disturbance in the world around us.

A wave is a vibration of energy. A particle is mass and forms the building blocks of everything we see around us. Note the apparent diametrically opposed properties of each.

In Thomas Young's time, quantum theory hadn't been invented. He performed his experiment to prove that Newton was wrong in asserting that light was made up of little particles. Young averred that light travelled through the ether as waves. To prove it he shone a beam through a metal sheet with a slit in it and a vertical band of light appeared on a screen, which had been placed behind the slit. So far so good – just what you would expect.

He then shone the light through two parallel slits and, instead of getting two parallel bands he got something looking like an oversized bar-code – bands of light and shade. Young was delighted at this because it proved that the light had passed through the slits as waves because it had formed what is known as an 'interference pattern', and was behaving just like the waves he had created in a tank of water when he conducted an earlier experiment. An 'interference pattern' is always caused when waves spread out after passing through the slits and collide with one another. So far in the experiment, everything had gone to plan and he had proved Newton wrong. Light was definitely made of waves.

But over a century later, well after Quantum Theory was invented, scientists decided to see what would happen if they 'fired' particles through the slits, like a gun shooting marbles. For ease of use they employed photons, particles of light. When one slit was fired at, things went just as expected – a vertical bar appeared. BUT...when they used both slits, instead of the expected two bars, an interference pattern materialised. How could this be? How could a particle – a little piece of matter - behave like a wave?

To try to work it out, baffled physicists decided to fire

one photon at a time so it couldn't be suggested that the particles were bouncing off each other and causing the bands. The mystery deepened; an interference pattern manifested itself again. The particle behaved as if it was going through one slit while its ghostly twin was passing through the other and interfering with itself. Now here is where the relevance to dowsing comes in. Determined to get to the bottom of this enigma, the experimenters placed a detector next to the front of one opening to see which slits the 'real' single photon actually went through.

The result was beyond their imagination. When observed, the particle reverted to type and behaved just like a little marble going through just one slit and creating a single, vertical band. No interference pattern in sight. It seemed that the very act of observing it had caused the photon to go though just one slit, not both. What had happened to its ghostly other self? The photon had apparently decided to act like a particle and not a wave, as though it was aware of being watched. When the scientists stopped watching the interference pattern reappeared! It seems the scientists' minds had determined how reality had unfolded.

So, what is matter? Particles or waves? It would seem that both Newton and Young were correct – light can be BOTH particles and waves. Matter exists as waves of probability until the observer (human consciousness) causes, in science jargon, a collapse of the wave function and reality appears. For some unknown reason that haunts scientists, everything we perceive as having mass is just a wave of information (or possibilities) until we observe it in some way. The Double-Slit Experiment shows us that dowsers create reality just by dowsing for it (observing).

So, do dowsers of subtle energies actually create what they are looking for? By focusing their minds and bringing their rods/pendulums/forked sticks into play are they causing infinite probabilities to coalesce into one reality? And is that reality a product of their own consciousness or are they acting in partnership with the Cosmic Creator? While it's just possible to believe that in some way dowsers manipulate the unseen energies all around us, what about the creation of physical objects like streams, or archaeological remains, that have probably been there for hundreds of years?

Does the same principle – the observer creates reality – apply to solid objects? When dowsers search for water 200 feet under the ground, is the water there or is it being created? Of course the water is there, you will reply. It's obvious that a stream has been trickling its way across the geological strata for aeons and dowsers eventually detect it. That is the conventional view. But, looked at through the prism of the Quantum Universe, the stream has only been there for eons because it 'knew' it was to be created by human consciousness out of the waves of a million possibilities. It was there because, one day, a dowser (or some other conscious being) was destined to find it. The Divine Plan is already nascent, worked out in every detail. It waits only for us to bring it to life.

Preposterous? Perhaps, but evidence of this radical viewpoint can be found in a sequel to the dreaded Double-Slit Experiment – the Delayed Double-Slit Experiment. Back to the questing mind of John Archibald Wheeler. He set up detectors the other side of the slits to monitor which slit the particle had actually gone through after it had made its choice. The results were astounding. Whichever photon or electron was detected AFTER it had passed through the slit always behaved as a particle. Not a wave in sight. But those that were not being monitored behaved as waves!

The inescapable conclusion was that the particle 'knew' before it even reached the slit that it was going to be observed, so it obediently behaved as a particle. It seemed that somehow it had read the scientists' minds. Or perhaps it was just playing its part in a pre-destined scenario. A variation on this experiment has been done hundreds of times since, using state-of-the-art equipment, including laser beams, beam splitters and a device called the 'electron biprism', always with the same results. The 'observation', involving the participation of human consciousness, causes reality to jump into being.

But, is it really possible that dowsers can 'create' such solid matter as archaeological remains, or an underground stream just by detecting it? How could this be? How could the ruins of a Roman palace (and, by implication the glories of the Roman empire itself) only exist courtesy of human consciousness engaging with it some time in the future? Here we come back to the co-creation theory. It works perfectly if you can accept that everything is pre-ordained and that life in this dimension unfolds to a Cosmic Plan, which requires human consciousness as a co-creator. The prescient particle above was not reading any minds. It was merely playing its part in the timeless, cosmic drama. Admittedly, this idea is a tall order for those who believe in the concept of free will. But a universe unfolding to a meticulous plan is a notion supported by science.

Proposing a variation of the above Delayed Choice research Professor Wheeler pointed out that astronomers could perform the same experiment on light from quasars, those extremely bright, mysterious objects found near the edges of the universe. The experiment requires a 'gravitational lens', which is provided by a galaxy or other massive object. This gravitational lens splits the light from the quasar and then refocuses it in the direction of a distant observer, creating two or more beams of light.

The astronomers' choice of how to observe the quasar's photons here in the present determines which path each photon took billions of years ago! Wheeler's thought experiment has since been demonstrated in a laboratory. In 1984 physicists at the University of Maryland used a light source and an arrangement of mirrors to provide a number of possible photon routes. It was clearly demonstrated that the paths the photons took were not fixed until the experimenters made their measurements, even though those measurements were performed after the photons had already left the light source and had begun their circuit through the trail of mirrors.

Wheeler conjectured that we are part of a universe that is a work in progress; as it observes itself it is building itself. It is not only the future that is still undetermined but the past as well. When we peer back into time, even all the way back to the Big Bang, our present observations select one out of many possible quantum histories for the universe. So, in the delayed choice experiment either the light 'knew' it was destined to be observed by a human consciousness far into the future, and behaved accordingly, or its behaviour was predestined as part of a Grand Cosmic Plan, in which we are co-creators.

Either way, dowsers (and of course us lesser mortals) are playing our part in the destiny of the planet.

ABOUT THE AUTHOR

In my career as a BBC journalist and broadcaster and a national and regional journalist, I'd written my fair share of stories about The Unexplained which piqued my interest in the paranormal. This led me to membership of the widely-respected Society for Psychical Research, and the British Society of Dowsers where I learned the art of divining. After establishing the Guernsey Society of Dowsers, I went on to focus my dowsing skills on the areas of Health and Subtle Energies. I later taught dowsing at the Guernsey College of Further Education and I still run workshops on both dowsing and energy healing.

Through all my many years of researching the metaphysical, esoteric, mystical, occult, paranormal, the Mysterious and Things That Go Bump in the Night I've come to the conclusion that The Unconscious Mind is the one factor common to them all. Which means that everyone has access to psychic or so-called paranormal powers. This is now my mission – to encourage everyone to use their sixth sense to fulfil their potential. I found dowsing to be a practical way of harnessing the energies we've talked about in this book. If you want to learn more I'd recommend (I would, wouldn't I?) my beginners' guide *Dowse Your Way To Psychic Power* available on any Amazon site worldwide. Just put Anthony Talmage in the books search field.

If you do this you'll find other books I've written – a complete contrast to the world of the metaphysical which we've been journeying through together here, in that they are modern thrillers. My first venture into fiction was a radio play, an occult thriller *'Ghost in the Machine'*, broadcast in South Africa and Ireland. I've now followed that up with two novels *Ticket to a Killing*, a 'Woman in jeopardy' thriller featuring reporter Emma Holgate, and *The Kirov Conspiracy* in which the hero is a media boss, Paul Scott, who uncovers a scheme by a Russian mobster to use drugs money to help fund Putin's war in Syria. I now have plans for other works of fiction, based on my experiences both in the media and in the field of the supernatural.

BIBLIOGRAPHY

Elizabeth Mayer *Extraordinary Knowing*, Bantam Dell Publishing Group 2008

George Applegate *The Complete Guide to Dowsing*, Vega Books 2002

Anthony Talmage *Dowse Your Way To Psychic Power*, Amazon 2015

T C Lethbridge *The Power of the Pendulum*, Routledge & Paul 1976

Edith Fiore *The Unquiet Dead: A Psychologist Treats Spirit Possession*, New York: Ballantine Books 1987

Carl Wickland *Thirty Years Among the Dead*, National Psychological Institute 1924. This is the definitive, classic work laying the foundations for all future investigations into the nature of earthbound spirits.

William J. Baldwin *Healing Lost Souls: Releasing Unwanted Spirits from Your Energy Body*, Charlottesville, VA: Hampton Roads Publishing 2003

Hazel Courteney *Divine Intervention*, Amazon 2011

Rupert Sheldrake *A New Science of Life,* Park Street Press 1995

Rupert Sheldrake *Dogs That Know When Their Owners Are Coming Home,* Three Rivers Press 2000

Jean Slatter *Hiring the Heavens,* New World Library 2005

Hans Andeweg *In Resonance With Nature,* Floris Books 2009

Danah Zohar *The Quantum Self,* Harper Collins 1991

Kathe Bachler *Earth Radiations,* John Living 2007

Cleve Backster *Primary Perception: Biocommunications with Plants,* White Rose Press, illustrated edition 2003

Alexandra David-Neel *Magic and Mystery in Tibet,* University Books 1965

Michael Talbot *The Holographic Universe* Harper, Perennial 1992

Adrian Incledon-Webber *Heal Your Home,* Amazon 2013

Masaru Emoto *Messages from Water,* Hay House 2010

Hamish Miller & Paul Broadhurst *The Sun and the Serpent,* MYTHOS 4th edition 2003

Allan Kardec *The Spirits Book,* Spastic Cat Press 2012 (re-issue)

G M Glaskin *Windows of the Mind: The Christos Experience,* Prism Press 1986

18075794R00121

Printed in Poland
by Amazon Fulfillment
Poland Sp. z o.o., Wrocław